CROWNED
WITH
VICTORY

Four Forgotten
Irish Firebrands

AMBASSADOR

BELFAST ◆ GREENVILLE
NORTHERN IRELAND ◆ SOUTH CAROLINA

CROWNED WITH VICTORY
This compilation first published 1998

Copyright © 1998 Ambassador Productions Ltd.

ISBN 1 84030 037 X

Ambassador Publications
a division of
Ambassador Productions Ltd.
Providence House
16 Hillview Avenue,
Belfast, BT5 6JR
Northern Ireland

Emerald House
1 Chick Springs Road, Suite 203
Greenville,
South Carolina 29609, USA

www.emeraldhouse.com

LisT
OF
CONTENTS

TOM HAIRE
"THE PRAYING PLUMBER"
BY A. W. TOZER 7

GIDEON OUSELY
"THE IRISH WESLEY"
BY LEONARD RAVENHILL 25

ANN PRESTON
"HOLY ANN"
BY HELEN BINGHAM 31

✗ BILLY SPENCE ✗
"A TROPHY OF GRACE"
✗ BY JAMES GRUBB 107 ✗

TOM HAIRE
"THE PRAYING PLUMBER"
BY A. W. TOZER

❖

A SKETCH OF THE PRAYING PLUMBER

You have only to glance at his round red face and his twinkling blue eyes to guess the place of his birth. And when he smiles and says, "Guid marnin," there is no doubt left. Tom Haire is Irish.

Tom is not just somewhat Irish; he is so completely identified with the looks and ways and speech of the Emerald Isle that nothing on earth can ever change him. His soft, thick, almost fuzzy brogue reminds you of every Pat-and-Mike story you have ever heard, and then the happy upside-down construction that often comes out when he talks sounds like the best of John M. Synge.

For the purposes of this sketch I shall let Tom speak in ordinary American English, though I admit we may lose something by so doing. Tom is just a plumber, not a celebrity, so any interest he may arouse among Christians is bound to be spiritual. He will not see what is written until it appears in print; and if I know him as well as I believe I do he will not read it afterwards. Tom is like that.

The two characteristics to mark Tom Haire as unusual are his utter devotion to prayer and his amazing spiritual penetration. Three months after his conversion, when he was sixteen years old, he formed the habit of praying four hours each day. This practice he followed faithfully for many years. Later he added one all-night prayer session each week. In 1930 these weekly all-night prayer times were increased to two, and in 1948 he settled down to the habit of praying three nights of every week. He gets along on very little sleep. In addition to the three nights each week that he stays awake to pray he is frequently awakened in the night seasons by a passage of Scripture or a burden of prayer that will not let him rest. "And almost always," he says, "the Lord wakens me early in the morning to pray."

ONE OF HIS SECRETS - NEARNESS TO GOD

Tom Haire is a rare compound of deep, tender devotion, amazing good sense and delightful sense of humour. There is about him absolutely nothing of the tension found in so many persons who seek to live the spiritual life.

Tom is completely free in the Spirit and will not allow himself to be brought under bondage to the rudiments of the world nor the consciences of other people. His attitude toward everyone and everything is one of good-natured tolerance if he does not like it, or smiling approval if he does. The things he does not like he is sure to pray about, and the things he approves he is sure to make matters of thanksgiving to God. But always he is relaxed and free from strain. He will not allow himself to get right-eously upset about anything. "I lie near to the heart of God," he says, "and I fear nothing in the world."

That he lies near to God's heart is more than a passing notion to Tom. It is all very real and practical. "God opens His heart," he says, "and takes us in. In God all things are beneath our feet. All power is given to us and we share God's almightiness." He has no confidence at all in mankind, but believes that God must be all in all. Not even our loftiest human desires or holiest prayers are acceptable to God. "The river flows from beneath the throne," he explains, "and its source is not of this world. So the source of our prayers must be Christ Himself hidden in our hearts.

Though he counts heavily on the power of prayer he has no faith in the virtue of prayer itself as such. He warns against what he calls "merit prayers," by which he means any prayer offered with the secret notion that there is some-thing good in it which will impress God and which He must recognise and reward. Along with "merit prayer" goes "merit faith" which is the faith we think will in some way please God.

"Too many of God's people are straining for faith," says Tom, "and holding on hard trying to exercise it. This will never do at all. The flesh cannot believe no matter how hard it tries, and we only wear ourselves out with our human efforts. True faith is the gift of God to an obedient soul and comes of itself without effort. The source of faith is Christ in us. It is a fruit of the Spirit.

He flatly rejects the notion that we "can buy something with prayer." "God's gifts come from another source," he insists. "They are 'freely given', and have no price attached. It is the goodness of God that gives us all things. God gives His free gifts generously to those of His children who bring themselves into harmony with His will. Then they have but to ask and He gives."

Brother Tom fasts quite often and sometimes the fast is prolonged for some time. But he scorns the thought that there is any merit in it. "Some people," says Tom with a shake of the head, "Some people half kill themselves by ascetic practices. They imagine God to be so severe that He enjoys seeing them hungry. They go about pale and weak in the mistaken belief that they are making themselves dear to God. All such notions come from the flesh and are false." Once during a prolonged season of prayer he got suddenly thirsty and without qualm of conscience broke off prayer and went out for a cup of tea. This got him into difficulties with certain fellow Christians who felt that he was surrendering to fleshly appetites. But he has dwelt so long in the spacious heart of God that he is unaffected by the scruples of others. God's heart is no strait jacket even if some imperfectly taught saints insist on acting as if it were. "Where the Spirit of the Lord is, there is liberty."

Wherever there is a strain in the life we may be sure the flesh is operating. The Holy Spirit gives fruitful burdens but never brings strain. Our very eagerness to have our prayers answered may cause us to lapse into the flesh if we are not watchful. So Tom reasons. A women sent for him recently and wanted him to pray for her healing. She was in a very bad condition, but Tom would not pray. He detected in her eagerness to get well a bit of rebellion against the will of God. So he set about breaking her rebellion down. "Sister," he asked innocently, "and have you ever read the Scripture, 'Precious in the sight of the Lord is the death of His saints'? Sure, and you would not want to rob the Lord of all that preciousness, would you?" It was his way of telling her that she was not fit to live unless she was willing to die. The shock had its intended effect, and after some further conversation Tom felt that the woman had surrendered her will to God. Then he prayed for her healing.

Anything that begins or ends in self is extremely hateful to Tom Haire. Self-righteousness, self-confidence and every other self-sin must be slain within us if we are to grow in the love of God. He goes back to the sixth chapter of Romans for his theology and insists that the doctrine become real in the life. To Tom the sanctified life is one that is dead indeed unto sin and alive unto God through Christ Jesus.

"A man is dead," he says, "when he no longer resists the will of God in anything. Dead men do not resist. You must go to God as a lamb, to obey, follow and die." Brother Tom sees a close relationship between dying and giving. "We must come to God with our hands open. A man can't be crucified while he keeps his fists closed. Open your hands in generous giving and hold nothing back. Even tithing can be harmful if we unconsciously feel that the one tenth we have given is all that belongs to God. Everything is His; we own nothing at all. The tenth is only the amount we set aside for religious work. The other nine tenths are His also, but He graciously permits us to use it as we have need."

KNOWLEDGE ON THE EXPERIENTIAL PLANE

For sinners and for defeated Christians Tom Haire feels only pity and a great sorrow of heart, but toward sin itself his attitude is one of stern, unsmiling hostility. To him sin is the cause of all our human woe, the veil that shuts us out from the blessed presence of God. It is never to be tolerated in any form by anyone who wishes to follow Christ.

From his view of sin it naturally follows that he holds repentance to be indispensable to salvation. His usually mild language becomes sharp and imperious as he calls his hearers to forsake iniquity and turn to God. For him there can be no compromise with wrongdoing. The seeking heart must make its eternal choice, either to serve sin and suffer the everlasting displeasure of God or to forsake all sin and enter into the divine fellowship through the mercies of Christ.

If you were to ask Tom what he considers the greatest hindrance to prayer he would answer instantly, "Unconfessed sin". And in coming to God the first thing to deal with is sin in the life. But for all that, it never enters his mind that he can atone for his sins by any kind of penance or self-punishment. Forgiveness is a free gift of God based upon the work of Christ on the cross and is never to be had on any other terms than faith. When a sin has been forsaken and confessed it is at that moment forgiven, never to be remembered against us forever. No possible good can come from brooding over it. It is gone for good.

Learned theologians have a fancy name for the doctrine of sin. They call it "hamartiology". In all probability Tom would not recognise the word if he chanced to come upon it, but his own hamartiology is fully adequate. He likes to recall that with God, forgiving and forgetting are the same thing. When God forgives, he forgets. Then Tom sums up his joyous personal theology in a single sentence, "If God forgets," he asks happily, "why should I remember?"

Tom has made two visits to the United States within the last few years. As he approached our shores for the first time he hid himself away on board the ship and sought the face of God in great earnestness to know what he should say to the "Amuricans". What God said to him, or what he seemed to hear God say to him, was so deep and

wise that it should   be seriously studied by every one
of us. Whether it was the very voice of God or only the
crystallization of a wisdom that had come to him through
long years of praying matters not at all. It is too wise and
wonderful to ignore.

"When you get to America," the Voice said within him,
"don't get mixed up in doctrinal trifles. Don't pay any
attention to their heads. Just look at their hearts. You will
find their differences to be of the head; their similarities
to be of the heart. So talk to their hearts. Don't read up on
the religious situation in America. Don't try to fit into things
or please people. Just talk to them straight out of your
heart. Tell them the things I have told you, and you will
get on all right." Fortunately Tom had the courage and
good sense to obey these wise admonitions.

Tom Haire, like many another uneducated man, takes
an attitude of meek deference toward all learning, and
gazes with great respect upon any man he considers
learned. But his confidence in his own kind of learning
makes him bold to speak out even in the presence of the
great. "My knowledge," he says, "has been all on the
experiential plane. I have never had the slightest interest
in theology as a mere theory. There is an anointing which
teaches all things so that we need not that any man teach
us." This attitude he holds in complete humility without
bigotry and without arrogance. Once I talked to him about
the views held by certain unbelieving intellectuals that
seemed to contradict his views. He advanced no arguments
to support his position. He bowed his head and spoke in a

low voice: "But they've never been where I've been," he said simply.

I have not felt free to ask Tom outright what books he has read. I only know that I have never seen him with any book except the Bible. It is altogether safe to assume that he has not read any of the devotional writers of the ages, yet his whole spiritual outlook is that of an evangelical mystic. There is a catholicity about him that would have made him completely at home with the great saints of the past. He could have preached to the birds along with Francis of Assisi (though his practical Irish mind would likely have inquired, "Shure, and what is the guid of it all?"). He might have sung across England with Richard Rolle, or sat in silence with George Fox or preached in a cemetery with John Wesley. And when the fiery logic of Charles Finney had devastated a congregation Tom might have come among the terrified seekers with his Bible and his wise words of instruction and led them straight to God.

The spiritual outlook of this twentieth century Irishman is so near to that of the fourteenth century Germans, Eckhart and Tauler, and the seventeenth century Frenchman, Fénelon, as to create a suspicion that he may be indebted to their writings for many of his ideas. But such is positively not the case. In all our dozens of conversations and our long prayer seasons together he has never so much as mentioned their names, nor has he ever quoted from their writings so much as one sentence. To him they simply do not exist. The only explanation for the remarkable resemblance between these Christian men so far removed in time is that the same Holy Spirit taught all of them, and where He can find listening ears He always teaches the same things. There is a unity of spiritual beliefs among men of the Spirit that jumps centuries, denominational gulfs and doctrinal hedges and perfects a communion of saints in spite of every effort of devil or man to keep them apart.

Probably the best commentary on the life and character of God's Irish servant is to say that after two years of rather intimate acquaintance with him I am unable to dig up anything of any consequence to write on the debit side of his life. I have seen him in the most trying circumstances, undergoing tests that would have tried the character of an angel, and I have not in one single instance seen him act otherwise than like a Christian.

Sometimes Tom can become very much of a tease. He particularly loves to josh his American friends about the inferiority of all things American to everything Irish. After his accident at a hotel fire in Chicago I went to see him often. He lay cruelly crushed by the long fall to the concrete pavement. His hip and thigh were fractured, his back broken in several places and one of his hands burned severely. He lay in what must have been harsh, grinding pain. To afford what assurance I could I bent close to his ear and told him that we had secured for him one of the beat orthopaedic surgeons obtainable. For all his great pain he managed a sly grin. "Ye mean he is one of the bust in Amurica," he whispered, "but don't forget, we have butter ones in Ireland."

Tom is not a finished speaker by any means, but in an average message he manages to throw off so many sparks of real inspiration that his hearers forget everything but the wonder of truth he is proclaiming. His messages tend to be circular, that is, they travel around to the same thought again and again. He reminds me of the advice given a young preacher to the effect that if he was going to harp on one string he should make that string a humdinger! Tom's string is love, fastened between the two pegs of faith and prayer. And that string is so long and so vibrant that it is seldom monotonous to listen to no matter how many times you hear it.

A LESSON ON "HOW TO RELAX WITH GOD"

Tom doesn't like to waste prayer. The habit of carefully surveying the situation before setting out to pray about things is characteristic of Tom Haire. To him prayer is a science whose laws can be learned. Praying itself is not a shot in the dark, not a net cast into the sea with the hope of a good catch. Praying is working along with God in the fulfilment of the divine plan. Praying is fighting close up at the front where the sharp deciding action is taking place.

According to Tom, there is such a thing as strategic prayer, that is, prayer that takes into account what the devil is trying to accomplish and where he is working, and attacks him at that strategic point. "Don't waste your time praying around the edges," he says. "Go for the devil direct. Pray him loose from souls. Weaken his hold on people by direct attack. Then your prayers will count and the work of God will get done."

Like many another plain believer who has sat at the feet of Christ longer than he has sat before books on theology, Tom tends to great simplicity in everything. All those fine shadings of truth that slow down so many highly educated persons are lost on Tom. To him there are just two forces in the universe, God and Satan, and if a specific phenomenon does not originate with one it will be found to have originated with the other. That may be oversimplification, but it puts an edge on his axe and gets results.

For one who fights as many battles as does this Irishman he is remarkably restful and self-possessed. Or better say, God-possessed, for his tranquillity is not natural; it is a divine thing. One of his favourite words is, "relax". He cannot see the good of tension anywhere. "Climb up into the arms of God," he says, "and relax. Getting things from God is as natural as breathing. When we pray we exhale; when we attack the answer we inhale. Prayer is simply a restful inhaling and exhaling in the Spirit of God."

It is significant that Dr. A. B. Simpson in his day taught the same truth in almost the same words. A stanza of one of his songs runs like this:

> *I am breathing out my longings*
> *In Thy listening, loving ears;*
> *I am breathing in Thy answers,*
> *Stilling every doubt and fear.*

Tom Haire never heard him preach nor read one of his books. It can only be explained as the same Spirit saying the same thing to different men who listen to His voice with equal care.

PRAYER AND POWER SHINING THROUGH DISASTER

It was four o'clock on a bitterly cold November morning when the telephone rang and an excited voice told me that the Norwood Hotel was burning and the guests were fleeing into the street in their night clothes to escape the flames.

Leonard Ravenhill, the English evangelist, and his prayer helper, Tom Haire, who were engaged in evangelistic meetings in our local church, were stopping at the Norwood. My informant could tell me nothing about these men. He only knew that some guests had died in the fire and others had been badly injured.

The logical place to look was St. Bernard Hospital, a few blocks away. There the scene was one of confusion. We stopped one of the hurrying sisters and inquired whether two Protestant evangelists had been admitted to the hospital in the last few minutes. The sister replied that she did not know. "But," she added, "as I helped to bring in one elderly man who had been hurt in the fire, he patted my cheek and asked me if I loved Jesus." We did not need to ask further. We had found Tom.

The weeks spent in St. Bernard Hosptial revealed the workings of God in many ways. Since this sketch concerns Mr. Haire I shall focus attention upon him mainly, though it should be said also that some of the experiences of Evangelist Ravenhill were not less wonderful.

It was not long before the news had spread through the hosptial that a Protestant "saint" had come among them. Nurses, doctors, supervisors and "sisters" of various kinds came to see Tom for themselves. Some of them admitted that they had not been aware that such men as Tom were still to be found running loose. Though their teachings forbade them to believe that Tom was a real Christian, their yearning hearts were better and more charitable than their dogmas, and they soon accepted him not as a Christian only but as a superior saint who could teach them the things of the Sprit.

Among those who visited Tom was a distinguished professor of philosophy at Notre Dame University. He came not to try to convert Tom but to hear from his mouth the wonders of a life of prayer and worship. In the course of his conversations he admitted that he was very much dissatisfied with the kind of Christian being produced within the Catholic fold. "They come to me and confess their sins," he said, "and then go back and do the same things again. I do not believe in that kind of religion. When a man comes to Christ he should come with John the Baptist repentance." This may sound trite to the average evangelical, but coming from a highly placed prelate of the Roman Church it is little less than astounding. And the whole experience suggests that there may be others enmeshed in the toils of Romanism who would look our way if we presented more examples of true godliness to catch their attention.

Tom's experience in the hospital was not without humorous incidents, though Tom was extremely careful never to give offence to the Catholic personnel. One Friday he suddenly developed an appetite for meat and called a nurse to him. "I say, suster," he began, "I crave a wee piece o' roast chucken. D'ye suppose ye cud get me some?" The nurse said No. It was Friday, and besides, chicken was not served to patients in that hospital. That was final. But Tom persisted. "But, suster. Ye don't know who I am! Tomorrah the British consul is comin' to see me. And besides that, look at the green light above me bed, put there in honour of auld Ireland. Now do I get some chucken?" Tom's blue eyes were twinkling. The consul's visit was scarcely to be in honour of Tom, and the green light above the bed surely had no remote relation to Tom's birthplace. The nurse left the room shaking her head doubtfully. After awhile she reappeared all smiles, and on a tray she carried a plate laden with roast chicken. Tom ate the meal with relish. He undoubtedly enjoyed it, but more than all he enjoyed the fact that he had gotten roast chicken in a Catholic hosptial on Friday.

One day as a supervisor was in his room, Tom suddenly asked her to pray for him. She promised she would go immediately to the chapel and say a prayer for him. But that would not do. "No," insisted Tom, "I want you to pray for me now. Right here." The surprised sister scrambled around in her voluminous bag and came up with a prayer book out of which she read a prayer. Then to be sure she would not leave, Tom grabbed her hand and hung on. "Now, suster, I'll pray for you." Then he launched into one of his tender, impassioned prayers while the sister stood reverently with bowed head. When he was through there was awe in her voice as she said, "That wasn't a memorised prayer, was it Tom?" That came right out of your heart. The Holy Ghost must have given you that." Until the day breaks and the shadows flee away it will not be revealed how much was accomplished through the suffering man of God by such faithful witnessing among persons who for all their blindness are at least reverent and serious-minded.

When the men were recovered sufficiently to be moved, a United States Army ambulance plane flew them to New York where they were the guests of the army for one day. Then they were flown overseas to their respective homes in England and Ireland.

In a few months, much improved physically, Tom came back to the United States. When all financial matters had been adjusted and the time was ripe to settle his accounts, Tom called on the doctor to pay the bill. The doctor looked him over and waited to hear what he would say. He had been told that he could request for a discount. He was definitely not prepared for what he was to hear.

"Now, Doctor," Tom began, "I want to settle up with you. I understand that you expect me to ask for a discount on my bill on the grounds that I am a Christian worker. But, Doctor, I shall do nothing of the kind. You see. I am connected with the Deity and I run my business on the same principles as God runs His. God never asks for discounts. His method is to give full measure, pressed down, shaken together and running over. And I want to do the same. Here is a signed cheque made out to you. Only the amount is left blank. Now you take it, write in any amount you please and it will be honoured. And I'd rather you made it too much than too little."

This was more than the Catholic surgeon could stand. He broke down and wept, threw his arms around Tom and kissed him like a son. "I have never seen a Christian like you before in all my life. Tom. Here, hand me the cheque." Then he deducted $250 from the total bill and wrote in the reduced amount.

While Tom was going through the long siege of suffering after his accident he was forced for the first time in years to give up his habit of praying three nights each week. He missed having these long seasons of intercession, but he did not let it bother him nor did he allow himself to get under bondage because he could not pray as before. God knew that His servant would be back at his regular habit as soon as he could, and Tom knew that He knew and understood. Between friends there are some things that can be taken for granted.

The doctors have told Tom that his accident has probably prolonged his life many years by forcing a long rest just at the period in his life when his heart was in need of it. Of course such a matter is in the hand of God and any prediction of longevity would be altogether rash and foolhardy. But one thing is sure: whether he stays among us for many years or slips off to heaven tomorrow is not of any consequence to Tom. He has lived so long on the portico of heaven that he will feel quite at home when the Father comes out and invites him inside.

GIDEON OUSELY
"THE IRISH WESLEY"
BY LEONARD RAVENHILL

❖

In 1762 John Wesley made his second invasion of the City of Galway in Ireland. Unknown to him, snug in his cradle in a corner of the same country lay a baby boy who, when Wesley had ceased his labours, would be beginning a ministry scarcely less effective and endued with the same baptism of fire. Gideon Ousely, for that was the name of this God-endued soul winner, was born in Dunmore, Ireland, on February 24, 1762.

His mother was careful to safeguard Gideon from his father's ideas on Deism. She had the boy read to her at nights from Tillotson's "Sermons" or Young's "Night Thoughts" and his "Last Day." Time did not erase these thoughts from the mind of the reader.

Gideon was first awakened to his lost estate by a man who was a soldier fighting in two armies at the same time - the Fourth Royal Irish Dragoon Guards and the army of the Lord.

He was also deeply affected by the preaching of John Hurley and under his anointed exhortation he came into grace. In his twenty-ninth year in the middle of May, 1791, Gideon beheld "the Lamb of God slain for him" and felt that God had taken the load and darkness away and had bestowed the long-sought peace.

At the "Class meeting" John Hurley asked him, "Do you believe that the Lord has pardoned you?"

"Yes," he replied, "my soul doth magnify the Lord, and my spirit doth rejoice in God my Saviour."

Later, over the Irish countryside, as dumb beasts would look over the fences, they heard the singing soul of the horse-borne preacher, eloquent and loud in his praises to the One who, as Wesley put it, "Saved poor souls out of the fire and quenched their brands in Jesus' blood."

The Irish preacher of whom I write had but one eye. Yet no man with two eyes ever saw more clearly from the divine record that men are lost now and lost forever except they repent, than did this man. Men to him were not men, but spirits wrapped in flesh-souls for whom Christ died. He saw them as potential jewels for the diadem of Christ or fuel for the flames of hell.

Sparks flew from the hoofs of his flying horse with its foam-trimmed mouth and sweating flanks as he sped with pitiful urgency on those rough Irish roads. One would think that this preacher had had a preview of hell or a secret note delivered by Gabriel himself that the end of the age would come within the next twenty-four hours. Such was his quenchless zeal for souls. There can be no doubt about it that this blessed man could say, "The zeal of thine house hath eaten me up."

Neither Paul Revere of America or John Gilpin of England ever rode with more zeal than this "Irish Wesley" as some have called him. It might be nearer the mark to class him with England's Whitefield or America's Gilbert Tennent. He was their kinsman in spirit. He belonged to the fellowship which leaps ecclesiastical labels - the fellowship of the burning heart.

In London, St. Paul's Cathedral has a pulpit in impressive marble. In his City Road Chapel, Wesley had a nice polished mahogany pulpit. Jesus used the rim of a well for a pulpit. Our hero had for his pulpit often times a pair of stirrups or a backless saddle.

Consider the scope of one of Ousely's prayer-baptised missionary journeys among the unlettered Irish folk of the then wild countryside. See these things happen. A priest stands waiting for the wedding party to enter the church. When the carriage bringing the happy couple arrives, our hero preacher walks to them. He gently warns them of eternity, and, in a few minutes, the happy couple are startled to find themselves involuntarily kneeling on the ground while the flaming evangelist prays for them. He then rushes on. Over the cemetery wall he espies weeping souls, wailing and affrighted because their loved one has gone - whither? He lifts his great voice in prayer above their flesh-freezing cries.

Next see Ousely in the market place. This is the scene of a last public execution. Thousands are gathered. I believe it was our preacher who climbed the scaffold and ministered to the shaking criminal. After he had led the man to Christ, the preacher with the scaffold for a pulpit, bombarded the crowd with the facts of eternal solemnity. As he spoke, the body of the dead was swinging from the scaffold. Within sight of death he preached to the careless sinners of eternal life. As he pictured for them the eternal woes of those who die without God and without hope, he turned their dancing into mourning.

One who heard Ousely testify said later, "I wish I could reproduce his testimony as I heard it. The solemnity and loving earnestness of his manner, the melting tone of his voice, the beaming look, the grateful joy, the flowing tears, the impassioned character of his appeals, cannot be reproduced on paper."

Gideon took more than one preaching tour of England. There, as in Ireland, he saw the manifest power of the Lord, evidenced not only in striking conversions, but also in phenomena. Folk would fall into a swoon while he preached. Some would appear to be dead and respond neither to gentle attention nor to shouting and shaking. Later they "awoke" and entered into the peace of salvation.

The flaming soul was driven from the market place and derided from pulpit. Priests and Protestants alike sought to put road blocks in the way of this advancing crusader. On he pushed.

His spirit was willing, though at times his flesh was weak. But he drove it on. Rough riding, rough eating, rough sleeping, and rough crowds in the markets all made draining demands upon him. Yet in his 75th year he was still street preaching and holding the attention of the crowds as he urged them sometimes in English and at other times in eloquent Irish, but always with impassioned earnestness to "flee from the wrath to come."

In his 76th year (note this well, preacher) he says, "I preached six and thirty times in sixteen days" He later records, that "from Sunday morning, August 27, to Thursday morning, September 21, I was enabled by my Lord to preach fifty-four times in and out of doors - not far off from my seventy-seventh year!"

A year short of his eightieth birthday, Gideon Ousely died - full of wisdom, full of years, full of grace. Devout men carried him to his resting place, a grave on Mount Jerome, and "there returned to mother earth all that was now earthly of one of the best sons of Erin that the green sod ever covered."

ANN PRESTON
"HOLY ANN"
BY HELEN BINGHAM

❖

A FOREVIEW

She was Irish, and a saint. The terms may to some minds seem incongruous and may not generally be associated. Hot Celtic blood may possibly not be easily turned into the channel of sanctity, but nevertheless Ireland has had its saints, and Ann Preston was one. She might not be able to claim lineal descent from St. Patrick, and to be sure saintliness does not always descend a family tree. But then she was connected with the same source of life, for "He that sanctifieth and they that are sanctified are all of one."

She was Irish, anyway; there could be no doubt about that. Although she had not trodden the green sod of the

Old Land for well-nigh seventy years, her face had not lost anything of the national characteristic, and to hear her speak but a few sentences would have settled that question beyond the suspicion of a doubt.

And then she was a saint; at least so everybody said that had ever known her, and she was known to thousands, and her influence felt far beyond the limits of any common life. There was surely something remarkable in the career of a poor woman, when at its close all ministers of all denominations gathered around the casket bearing the lifeless remains, and one of our large city churches was packed to the doors to listen to the testimony of those representing all branches of the Church, as they bore witness that the life of this sainted woman had been an untold blessing to them. There would have been nothing strange had the coffin contained the remains of one of the earth's great ones. Culture or wealth has an attractive power, but this woman was unlettered, illiterate. She had no wealth to bequeath, and not a living relative to mourn her loss. She had lived during the last years like Elijah, as the guest of a poor widow, who ministered to her needs. Her very coffin was a gift of love, and her dust was deposited in the lot of another.

On the following Sunday the Mayor of Toronto testified in his church, "I have had two honours this week. It has been my privilege to have an interview with the President of the United States. This is a great honour. Then I have been pallbearer to Holy Ann." And no reflection was cast upon the head of the great Republic when he added, "Of the two honours I prize the latter most."

A life with such an influence is surely worthy of some memorial, and it has been our endeavour to so set forth the authentic records that she, being dead, may yet speak, and that the testimony which she bore may continue to bless the lives of those who read it. We would fain hope that the story may prove an antidote for the materialism and unbelief of our day, as the facts recorded bear emphatic testimony to the inerrancy of the Word of God and furnish abundant evidence that behind that Word God still lives to make its every promise sure. On no other ground shall we find the explanation of the mysteries wrapped up in the life of our Irish saint.

NINETY YEARS AGO

That saintship did not come by natural generation in the case of Ann Preston is very evident from the fact that at the time of her birth neither her father nor mother made any pretension to piety. In fact, it would seem that they had little to do with religious things in any shape or form. Her home was one of those typical Irish shanties in the secluded village of Ballamacally, just about a mile from the little town of Markethill, in the County of Armagh.

We do not care to paint the house any prettier than it really was, or dress it in any way with poetic fancy. The thatched roof was just as sombre as that of any other cottage, and the usual stack of peat did not enhance the beauty of the landscape. Moreover, the pig-pen was in just as close proximity to the back door as custom and convenience permitted an Irishman to have it. In those days there were no haunting dreams of germs and microbes, and the grunt and squeal were not out of harmony with the usual music of the household. James Preston was a hard-working man; at least he laboured for long hours in his occupation as a herdsman. Then after the day's toil it was necessary for him to spend the evening hours in tilling the little potato patch attached to his cottage. Even the women had to take their share of this kind of work in order to keep hunger away from the door.

Ann was fortunate having two older sisters to sing her lullabies; but to compensate for this bit of good fortune, after nursing two sisters and a solitary boy that made their appearance later, Ann was hired out to rock the cradle in a neighbour's home.

When asked for her childhood reminiscences two things seemed to have left their imprint, one upon the mind, and the other may have made more impression in other ways at the time, for she quaintly concluded her story by adding, "I mind that for the whipping I got."

It is natural that the entrance of death into any home should leave an indelible mark upon the child mind, and Ann recalled the dissolution of a godly aunt who was sent to bless them for a short time. Beneath that humble roof she had witnessed a good confession, and in that closing scene it was manifest that "Blessed are the dead that die in the Lord." Ann was too young to think much of eternal things then, but her older sister Mary dated the beginning of a new life to that Providence that brought the influence of this aunt to their home.

The other memory of childhood - that is, of the very early days - took her back over ninety years. Wholesome chastening should leave a long impression. Pity the child whose waywardness is not marked by the memory of some rebuke or correction. When not more than five years of age Ann's mother took her down by the little stream that meandered near by the village, and left her in charge of some cotton which she was bleaching on the banks. Her instructions were very clear. On no account was she to leave the spot or lose sight of the goods. Even amid the honesty of old Ireland some caution was necessary.

But Ann was a real child of Eve, and the forbidden thing became the attractive thing. Her tempter came in the shape of a young girl, who just wanted Ann to run across the fields to her house to get something for her. This seeming friend would not take Ann's first refusal, but prevailed by promising watchful care of the cotton in her absence. Ann sped across the intervening space as fast as her legs would carry her, but when she returned from her errand she found that girl and cotton were both missing, and she was left alone to the flogging that followed.

Ann's education began and ended in little more than a week, but in that time she exhausted the patience of the teacher to the point of despair, and finally, after many vain attempts to teach her the first letters of the alphabet, he gave her a significant tap upon the head as he pathetically remarked before the class, "Poor Ann! She can never learn anything." And with this she was sent home in disgrace. Whether her case was absolutely hopeless we do not know, but her education terminated in this abrupt way.

However, if her mind was vacant, her bones were not lazy, and she saw little respite from work. In the family with which she was at once hired, the father herded cattle for a living. On Sunday, in order to allow him to carry on his devotions, the hired girl was deputed to herd the cattle, and Ann's week of toil was followed by a long day in the fields, where, in order to fight off the tremendous temptation to sleep at her task, she used to occupy herself in piecing quilts. This, of course, did not help her into a life of saintship. Compulsory Sabbath-breaking was not a very good beginning.

But this was only the commencement of evils. Her master kept a number of servants, and they were not of the immaculate type. The absence of master and mistress was usually a signal for an evening's fun and frolic, and their festivities were considered incomplete without a good supply of Irish whiskey. For some reason Ann had a horror of the fire-water. She may have seen some of its brutalising effects in her home surroundings, but, however that may be, she persistently refused to drink with the other hired help on these occasions.

Whether sunken into that terrible condition of depravity which takes delight in seeing others indulge in evil, or whether simply stung by the reproof of her refusal, they determined to force her to take part with them. By sheer strength some held her down while the others poured the liquor down her throat, and then with diabolical delight they made sport of her as she sat helplessly appealing to them to put her to bed, mumbling over and over again in her intoxicated state, "Fitter I was saying my prayers than sitting here drunk."

Just about this time a well-meaning effort was made to impart to her some religious instruction, but it failed as ignominiously as the attempt to teach her letters. A good Methodist sister undertook to teach her the Lord's Prayer, but was shocked at the revelation of ignorance when she commenced. She said to Ann, "Now, repeat it after me, 'Our Father which art in heaven,'" and Ann at once followed in parrot-like fashion, "Now, repeat it after me, Our Father which art in heaven." But when constant repetition failed to make the least impression on the memory, this good friend finally abandoned the task in despair.

THE GREAT CHANGE

For four years Ann continued in this situation, and then seemed to fall into worse surroundings, for after six months in her next home she was actually contemplating taking a situation with the low saloon keeper of the place. God very graciously arrested her downward steps, and providentially opened a situation for her with a Christian mistress. Mrs. McKay hated the liquor, for her husband had been driven to the asylum through it, and while he was at this time at home once more, yet her strong dislike to the intoxicating cup was often expressed, and Ann was certainly fully warned along this line. Her goodness was not merely that of the negative kind, for she had positive piety of the warm Irish Methodist type and she sought to influence all who came beneath her roof. Mrs. McKay observed family prayer, and Ann was invited to join them in worship. It was a new epoch in her experience, although her dull mind comprehended very little of what was being said. Her ignorance of religious matters may be judged from the fact that when asked to bring the New Testament she went and brought a newspaper. The book had never been used in any home that Ann had ever lived in, so that her ignorance was but natural.

Mrs. McKay was very anxious to win her hired help, but she acted quite judiciously in that for some time she omitted to press Ann to accompany her to religious meetings. She finally ventured to invite her to come to a class meeting. After a little pressure, Ann agreed to go. It was all so new to her that she looked on in open-mouthed wonder as she saw some weeping and others praising God. As things proceeded she seemed to be somewhat disgusted. To her it seemed like a religious cant. She even watched to see whether the crying was real, or whether they were wetting their faces. She hardly knew what to make of the whole matter.

After dinner that day the mistress rang the bell and Ann entered the parlour, and was surprised when she was invited to sit down. Mrs. McKay opened the conversation with, "Well, Ann, how did you like the class meeting?"

Ann's answer was a noncommittal, "I don't know," although if she had spoken her mind she would have called them a lot of hypocrites.

"Well," said Mrs. McKay, "won't you go again?"

Ann doggedly replied, "I don't think so."

When pressed for a reason, she stated that she had nothing to say in the meeting anyway. She felt utterly out of place when others were speaking and praying and weeping, while she sat as stolid as a post. In order to help her, Mrs. McKay suggested that she had some reasons to praise God, saying, "Who gives you food to eat and raiment to wear?" This well-meaning question missed the mark in Ann's mind, for while she made no reply, she had some big inward mental reservations which almost broke the ominous silence as she said to herself, "I guess I work hard enough for them."

Mrs. McKay got very little satisfaction that day, but she did not give up. The next Sunday she pressed Ann to go and hear a Mr. Armstrong Halliday. At this time the Methodists were very much despised and too poor to erect a place of worship; consequently meetings were held in private homes. On this notable Sunday the parlour was crowded and Ann was very glad to be out of range of the minister's eye. She remembered nothing that was said except the text, which was not one that would strike the average sinner. The words were, "Thou, when thou prayest, enter into thy closet, and when thou hast shut the door pray to thy Father who seeth in secret, and thy Father who seeth in secret shall reward thee openly."

Between eight and nine o'clock that evening, after the day's work was finished, Ann made her way up to the attic. It was just a bare room, the only furniture being a large wooden chair. Ann hardly knew why she did it, but she voluntarily knelt for the first time in her life and began to cry out without any conception of what was the matter. She lost all control of herself, and her mistress heard the noise down three flights of stairs. To her daughter she said, "Ann is taking the minister's advice," and a little while after she went up and asked Ann what was the matter. Ann looked up and answered, "I don't know, ma'am". But just then she seemed to have a sudden revelation of her trouble, and she added, "Oh, yes, I do. I see all the sins that ever I did from the time I was five years old all written on the chair in front of me, every one." And then, as she looked down, she cried out, "Oh, ma'am worse than all, I see hell open ready to swallow me." Then, like one of old, she began to smite her breast, and without any knowledge that she was repeating Scripture, cried out, "God be merciful to me, a sinner." Once more she became desperate, as she cried over and over again for mercy.

Mrs. McKay tried to hush her up, saying, "Don't let the master hear you." She suggested Ann should go to her own room and pray, and said, "I will go to mine and pray for you. " But Ann was too much in earnest for this, and said, "I don't care ma'am, if all the world hears me; I must cry for mercy." .

After a little while she retired to her room, but conviction did not cease, and she continued to pray until twelve o'clock, when she jumped up, saying, as she rose, "No mercy, Lord, for me?" But her heart was assured even as the question passed her lips, and Ann always said that as she looked up she saw the Saviour as He was on Calvary, and knew right then that His blood atoned for her sins.

She had the Methodist way of expressing it when she said, "I felt then something burning in my heart. I just longed for the morning that I could go home and tell my father and mother what the Lord had done for me." She went over to the table and picked up a Testament which the young ladies used, and then prayed her first simple request as a child of God. " O Lord, " she said, "you that has taken away this awful burden, intolerable to bear, couldn't you enable me to read one of these little things?" Putting her finger on a verse. The text was, "Whosoever drinketh of this water shall thirst again, but whosoever drinketh of the water that I shall give shall never thirst."

Our readers may believe it or disbelieve it, but for the first time in her life Ann was able to read a verse of Scripture. She did not get the whole verse, but, as our later narrative will show, this was the beginning of Divine assistance in the teaching of an ignorant girl.

The next morning Ann had her first opportunity of testimony. In the first place, she was sent to the tavern for the daily supply of beer for her master. It did not occur to her that this was inconsistent for a Christian, but when she entered the saloon she saw a mother giving her child a drink of whiskey. Even the tavern-keeper's wife protested at this, and said, "Don't give that poison to the child." Ann at once stepped up and said, "Well, ma'am, what makes you keep the poison?" The poor woman answered, "I wouldn't have it in the house if I could help it, but I can't, as my husband will sell it." This was Ann's first word of protest against evil.

Later in the day she managed to get home to tell her father and mother of her new-found joy. On the way the tempter suggested, "You don't feel the burning in your heart now. You had better not say anything about it till you are sure." However, she resisted the evil one, and with real fervour broke the news to her parents. They gave her a very cool reception. The only response from her mother was, "Oh, you are like your old grandfather; you are going out of your head." Not very encouraging, this, for a young convert. However, that very day she received a letter from her older sister Mary, who was working away off in Armagh, and she asked her mistress to read it to her. Ann did not remember any news conveyed in the letter except the one statement of her sister: "I am sure you have good news to tell me, Ann. I know by the answer that I have got in prayer." This illustrates the power of prayer, for Ann's sister had written the letter two days before. At that time Ann was utterly indifferent to religious influences, but by the time the letter reached her she had undergone the great change and had become a child of God.

STUMBLING UPWARDS

In her early Christian experience Ann was very much the child of circumstances, and her religious life was lived largely in the ebb and flow of feeling. How unsafe it is to base our hopes of heaven or our present relationship to God upon the trivial happenings of everyday life or the changing moods of the human mind. Of course Ann was not versed in the Word of God, and the only spiritual help she received was at the class meeting, where she listened to the experiences of others. This was doubtless of some help to her, but it could not take the place of thorough instruction in the truth.

As illustrating the kind of evidence that served to buoy up her life at this time, Ann tells the following little incident: One evening she had cleared out the ashes from the fireplace, but instead of leaving them by the grate until the morning, as was her wont, she took them out and set the box on the brick floor of the scullery. In the morning the box and part of the lid had been consumed by the fire, and at once Ann jumped to the conclusion that this was an evidence that she was saved and that God cared for her, for had she not taken the box out that evening the house would have been burned down.

There were evidently two ways of looking at the same thing, for this incident led Mr. McKay to discharge her, as he considered her unsafe and not to be trusted.

She had only been in her new situation a few months when Mr. Halliday, the minister under whom she had been converted, having evidently watched her industry, came to her one day and said that one of the best homes in his circuit needed a girl, and if she was prepared to go he would take her to the situation. Ann at once replied, "I will go anywhere, sir, where I can be free to serve the Lord." He took her to Armagh and introduced her to the family of Dr. Reid, with whom she was to spend many eventful years. He agreed to pay her the munificent wage of two dollars a month. Ann used to quaintly say, "The minister married me to Mrs. Reid," for he made Mrs. Reid promise that she would keep Ann as long as she would stay, and made Ann promise that she would stay as long as she would keep her, and concluded by saying, "It will not be long till I want you myself," as he was engaged to be married then. Many a time when dissatisfied and sorely tired with the difficulties of her situation, Ann would pack her little bundle ready to leave, but the remembrance of her promise always restrained her.

After Ann had been with Dr. Reid for some five years, he decided to go to Canada. He at once began to collect all his back debts. In those days there were no banking facilities, and he was compelled to keep all the money in the house. This was quite well known, and Ann was very nervous in being left alone in the home. They were away to the watch-night service at the coming in of the New Year, and Ann was alone with the baby. The approach to the house was guarded by two large gates, one of iron and the other of very heavy wood, and these were always kept locked. The back yard was surrounded by a very high stone wall, and things generally seemed very secure. At twelve o'clock that night Ann heard the iron gate shake, which was the usual signal of Dr. Reid's arrival. She was just about to go out and unlock the gate when she remembered that the service could not possible be over, and so she sat still. In a few minutes the noise occurred again, and a man climbed over the iron gate. Then, mounting a stack of turf, he managed to get over into the garden. Here the potatoes were kept, and he at once began to rob the pit. When her master came home Ann told them what had occurred, but her mistress made light of it. However, Ann insisted that this was a warning, and so impressed the doctor that he at once had the windows fixed with iron bars, and a large iron bolt put on the back door leading into the yard. Just two weeks after this, while the doctor was away out in the country attending a patient, Mrs. Reid and Ann were sitting up awaiting his return, when once more the same noise was heard. She was just about to go out with the key, when she was suddenly restrained, and said to Mrs. Reid, "O ma'am, this is the very same noise I heard two weeks ago." Her mistress asked, "Is the kitchen door locked?" Ann replied, "No," and with that she turned the key and pushed the long iron bolt across the door. She had hardly taken her hands off when the latch was lifted. Finding the door locked, the intruder evidently thought it to be a simple matter to burst the lock off, and stepping back he threw his full weight upon the door, but owing to the large bolt it would not yield. He tried again and again. The two women were naturally very much frightened. Ann began to pray, but Mrs. Reid suggested she go and call for help. Ann was afraid to venture out at the front door, but when it came to a choice of doing that or staying alone, she decided she would run for help.

The first place she called at the man would not come, and she went on to the barracks, but there was only one soldier in at the time, and he was on duty and refused to come. Finally she succeeded in reaching a home where they had not retired, and a big, burly fellow came out and at once offered to go with her, taking his revolver. They returned to the house just in time to meet Dr. Reid coming home. The would-be robber heard his usual signal and jumped over the wall, evidently with the intent of meeting Dr. Reid alone. However, when he discovered the two men in the darkness he turned and fled, but not before the doctor recognised him as a man he had occasionally hired to do odd jobs around the house.

The next day the man appeared at the doctor's office and said he was sorry to hear of the fright that Mrs. Reid had got the last night. The doctor in a very offhand manner replied, "Oh, that's no matter; sure, no one could get in here anyhow." Thinking the doctor did not identify him, the man went off, but otherwise Ann always felt that he had come with other intentions in mind that day.

It was in May that preparations were completed for their sailing, and Mrs. Reid asked Ann if she would go along with them to Canada. She replied, "Yes, for I can't break my promise to Mr. Halliday."

She went home to bid her parents good-bye. Her father was very much devoted to her, and at once said, "Ann, I can't let you go." But Ann insisted that she must, as she had already promised, and further said her ticket was already bought. Ann stayed at home all night, and then asked her parents to go a little way with her. After proceeding some distance down the road Ann turned around to address her father, but found he had suddenly disappeared to avoid the pain of saying goodbye. Her mother went on as far as Armagh, to where Ann's sister was living. Together they pleaded with Ann to stay at home, but Ann paid no attention to their entreaties. Her mother finally broke down completely, and wept as she said, "O Ann, I just can't let you go." In a very heartless and unfeeling way Ann turned and said, "I will go. Sure what's the difference? You won't live more than seven or eight years anyway." Many a time did these cruel words come back to Ann in the years that followed. She went on as far as Moy alone. Her mother and sister stood watching her for nearly two miles, and the look on the mother's face haunted her for many a long day.

FROM OLD WORLD TO NEW WORLD

Ann took ship at the Port of Londonderry. They were seven weeks on the water, and it must be remembered that in those early days not only was the voyage much longer, but the conveniences were not by any means such as to make an ocean trip enjoyable. The Reid family numbered seven, with two other relatives, and Ann had the care of the whole. There were no ship's cooks or stewards to minister to their wants. They carried their own supplies and cooked their own food. Ann had to serve three families. She says they were all very seasick. She was the only one that kept well throughout, and she, because, as she said, "Sure, I had no time to get seasick," managed to keep around the whole voyage.

The long journey had its usual incidents and Ann's duties furnished plenty of opportunity for unusual annoyances. She had to cook on the ship's ranges, and when her back was turned her pots were often set aside, and served the occasion for drawing out her Irish wrath. They dubbed her, "the praying-man's biddy," for her master used to hold family worship three times a day, much to the disgust of most of the travellers. Mrs. Reid only went up on deck once during the whole voyage, and on that occasion the ship gave a sudden lurch and a poor fellow who was up fixing the rigging lost his hold and fell, mangled and dead, upon the deck, almost at her feet. The nervous shock, combined with the seasickness, kept her in her berth during the rest of the voyage. This all made harder work for Ann. They met with several severe storms, and twice during the journey the passengers were fastened down below. On these occasions the despised praying-man was in great demand. Ann herself thought on one occasion that the end had come, and definitely committed herself to the Lord, expecting with the rest of the passengers that the boat would go down at any minute. However, piety prompted by danger is usually evanescent, and as soon as the waves calmed down the passengers returned to their old life of gambling, drinking and swearing.

In our day, with the ocean greyhounds to make the voyage so brief, the monotony of the ocean journey is sufficient to make land a welcome sight, and we can well imagine the delight with which, after being seven weeks out of sight of land, the passengers of one of the old sailing vessels would welcome the first glimpse. They entered the port of New York and sailed up the Hudson River. The beautiful scenery there was very refreshing after the ocean journey. From Albany they took the overland route and reached Toronto, then known as Little York. Here they tarried for a few months, and the doctor then moved to Thornhill and took up his practice in that place. The changing circumstances evidently had done little to assist the progress of Ann's religious life. At Thornhill at that period a very excellent lady, Mrs. Phoebe Palmer, led the class in the Methodist church, but while Mrs. Reid was in constant attendance, Ann could hardly be coaxed to go.

Ann was expected to look after the horse and buggy, and she had to attend to the robes. The doctor was very particular that these should be brought out at the last minute from the stove, so that they would be nice and warm for his journey. One day he saw Ann coming back to the house, having fixed the robes in the cutter some time before he expected to start. Evidently annoyed, he pulled Ann's hair as she went past him. Instantly Ann's temper blazed up, and snatching a big stick of wood that lay in the pathway, she threw it at him with all the force at her command. Fortunately it missed its mark. Evidently neither of them was very much edified by what followed, for not a word passed between them for the next two weeks, and at family prayer Ann used to put her fingers in her ears to keep out the sound of her master's voice. We do not wonder that at the class meeting Ann was diffident about getting up and giving her experience before Dr. Reid, who led her class and whose duty it was to give the young Christians fatherly advice and Christian counsel after they had narrated their experience. We cannot wonder that Ann was aggravated when the doctor used to conclude her narration by quoting an old Methodist hymn that ran thus:

"Your faith by holy tempers prove,
By actions show your sins forgiven,
And seek the glorious things above,
And follow Christ, your head, to heaven."

In spite of these untoward happenings, Ann did not give up the struggle to do that which was right, but she describes her life at this period as truly awful, sinning and repenting, sinning and repenting. She knew nothing of abiding rest. She used to often quote, when referring to this time, the old ditty that ran:

"'Tis worse than death my God to love,
And not my God alone."

However, through her struggles a kind hand was guiding her on to a place where she should not only enjoy greater blessing, but bear sweeter fruit.

DEFEAT TO VICTORY, OR THE SECOND GREAT CHANGE

We come to describe a great change in this life under consideration, and we do not wish to be misunderstood. A numerous body of Christians believe that Christian life can be divided into two distinct stages, the one summed up under the word "justification," and the other and further experience under the term "sanctification." In defining these states, however, great diversity of opinion is expressed. Some maintain that sanctification is something only to be experienced in the future state. Then among those who believe that sanctification is the present privilege of the Christian, two different views prevail - some contending that the experience consists in the entire eradication of the "old Adamic nature," while others contend that it is the state in which inward evil tendencies are entirely controlled or suppressed - but in the contention the one side too often gives evidence that there is need of a more perfect eradication, and the other that there is room for a more complete suppression. In this narrative, therefore, we are not contending for a theory, but simply narrating facts, and are frank to admit that we have witnessed the practical results which we are about to set forth in the lives of Christians taking either view of this great doctrine. In a general way we can appeal to our readers, and feel confident they will admit that in the circle of their acquaintances there are two classes of Christians. In the one there is not much to attract those who have never tasted of Christian joys. They live to all much under the cloud. It is true that they struggle to do right, and that there has been certainly a great change from their former life. They witness that their sins are forgiven. With actual wrongs committed there is speedy confession and repentance. They acknowledge their own powerlessness in the presence of temptation, and admit that they too often yield to some special besetment.

On the other hand, there is another class whose whole life and presence seems attractive. It is characterised by joyous victory. The soul has unbroken fellowship heavenward, and with its peace and joy it carries blessing wherever its influence is felt. The will is surrendered and the life wholly consecrated and the Divine acceptance is sealed by the filling of the Spirit. We shall not quarrel here as to how the transition is made from one state to the other. That those who have lived in the one should pass out of the first and into the second is sufficient for us. In other words, that the latter is possible by grace, is all that we desire to maintain.

In the case of Ann, who had been schooled among the Methodists, we cannot wonder that she largely dropped into their phraseology and more or less felt the impression of the teaching that prevailed. However, up to this time she knew very little of the teaching of John Wesley, and did not understand his theory of sanctification, and still less had she any corresponding experience. Her ungovernable temper was her great besetment. She wept over it, confessed it, fought with it, but all too frequently the whole process had to be repeated in the face of some great outbreak under specially trying circumstances. There came a change, however, and a time when she was delivered from its slavery. It happened thus: A young man who stayed all night at the home, before retiring led the family worship, reading Psalm 34. The 16th verse was strongly impressed upon Ann's mind: "The face of the Lord is against them that do evil, to cut off the remembrance of them from the earth." She requested the young man to mark it for her, and then went to her room and knelt down and prayed for light. She opened the Bible at the place where the leaf had been turned down, but the adversary was there to contend with her. His first suggestion was, "You can't read it," to which Ann relied, "Well, the Lord will give it to me," and in a wonderful way she was enabled to repeat it over and over again. Men may explain it as they will, but until this time, with the one exception already noted, Ann had never been able to read a word or decipher the alphabet, but from this time forth she could read in a simple way from the Bible, although until the close of life she was unable to read any other book and a newspaper was like a foreign language to her. While still upon her knees, she said, "Lord, what is evil?" And the answer came, "Anger, wrath, malice," etc. All night long she wept and prayed as the inward sinfulness was revealed to her. Toward morning in sheer desperation, she cried out, "O Lord, how will I know when I get deliverance?" The answer came, "Well, Jacob wrestled until he prevailed." In her simplicity, Ann asked, "What does 'prevailed' mean?" and to her the reply came, "Getting just what you come for and all you want." Again she queried,, "And what will it do for me when I get it?" The reply came back, "It will enable you to rejoice evermore, pray without ceasing, and in everything give thanks. You will live above the troubles of this world and the things that now upset you."

But other suggestions were interpolated from another source. Like a flash she recalled the circumstances of former outbreaks, and the suggestion came, "Yes, just wait until you are scrubbing the floor and the children come in with their dirty feet - then you will see." But the conviction deepened that these outbreaks of the carnal mind were displeasing to God, and that there was deliverance from them. When the morning broke and the children began to awaken, she was almost fleeing back to the bush to continue in her waiting for deliverance. She said determinedly, "I'll die, but I'll have it." She arose and went downstairs. To her overwrought mind the personal struggle with the adversary was so great that she could hear him following her. In the parlour she met the young man whose word had reached her heart. He asked her what she had been crying all night for, to which she replied, " I want to be sanctified throughout - body, soul and spirit." He simply said, "Well, Ann, how were you justified?" She replied, "Why, just by believing what God said." "Well," he said, "complete victory comes in the same way."

Again Ann went to prayer and pleaded the promise, "Ask and it shall be given you, seek and ye shall find, knock and it shall be opened unto you." She cried "Lord, I have been knocking all night. Open unto me! Open unto me!" And there is little doubt but that the answer came there and then. For two hours it seemed to her as though she had entered heaven. This time the family were aroused with her shouts of praise instead of her cries and groans. She said as she looked out that nature took on a different hue, and the very trees seemed to be clapping their hands and praising God. With her heart overflowing, she cried, "Father, didn't you intend that man should praise you more than these?" She at once began to tell it around. She went to her old class leader and made known her new-found joy. He bade her to rejoice evermore, and pray without ceasing in order to keep it. This brought in a shade of doubt, as she wondered how she could pray without ceasing. She thought of the absorbing affairs of life and the things that would occupy her mind, and wondered how such a thing was possible. But her mind was speedily set at rest by the Scripture passage, "Not slothful in business, fervent in spirit, serving the Lord."

Her joy was so great that she could not eat, and for eight days she was without food. Friends tried to persuade her to break her fast and to go forth and give her testimony, but it was some time before she felt that she could return to the ordinary duties.

For seven years and a half after this it just seemed as though she were living in heavenly places. She fell back on the Methodist Hymnal for expression, as she often cried:

"The opening heavens round me shine
With streams of scared bliss,
While Jesus shows His presence mine
And whispers 'I am His.'"

A NEW NAME

When Jacob had finished his all-night experience during which Jehovah broke the power of the carnal life within him, and brought him to the place of helplessness, where he could only cling to God and plead for blessing, he received a new name which described the changed life upon which he then entered. It is not to be wondered at that the life whose record we are now writing should at this time of wonderful change call for a new name. Just what length of time elapsed ere she received it we do not know. At first it was a term of derision. The Catholic boys scribbled in chalk-marks upon her door, "Holy Ann lives here. Go in and have a word of prayer." Gradually this term of derision clung to her, and even friends began to call her by the name. In her simple way, when she could no longer check the application of the word to her, she went to her closet and cried, "Oh, Father, they are calling me Holy Ann. Make me holy, so that the children will not be telling lies." By degrees this new name was so generally applied that for many years the greater number of her friends in all communities of Christians could not tell her proper name.

Some may demur at the acceptance of such a title, as though it involved spiritual pride, but we feel confident that were such a term to be applied to them its effect would be that of humiliation. It certainly did not cause Ann to become puffed up, although it did cause her, with the whole purpose of her life, to desire to fulfil the command of God. "Be ye holy, for I am holy." From this time forth there can be little doubt that the whole tenor of her life was changed, and wherever she went she became a faithful witness for God and an inspiration to all who knew her.

THE POWER OF PRAYER

This poor, ignorant woman had stepped from a life of struggling, marked too often by defeat, into a life of power and blessing - power not only manward, but into a life of wonderful intimacy with God and prevailing prayer. It was not long before this became generally recognised, and weaker Christians sought her counsel and begged her prayers, for it was very plainly seen that she had entered into the place where in a marvellous way she could "ask and receive", and where she had become a special subject of the thoughtful care of her Heavenly Father.

There was one incident that she has often told in some directions which has been received with doubt and sceptical unbelief, which beautifully illustrates this. We are confident that the facts are just as narrated. In jumping over a fence she twisted her foot and injured the ankle. It got worse and worse, until finally she was unable to walk around any longer. Dr. Reid said it would be necessary to scrape the bone. In these days, when such care is taken to relieve pain, we wonder how it was possible that Ann submitted to this painful operation without any anaesthetic, but, as she said, the Lord sustained her.

It was a long, long time before the wound healed up, and for over a year Ann was unable to walk. During this time of enforced inactivity she learned many precious lessons. She had become very weak through the great strain upon her system, and one day the doctor ordered her fresh eggs and milk. It did not occur to him that he was giving an impossible prescription, for it was in the dead of winter, and not a fresh egg was to be had anywhere in the village. All these matters were made subjects of prayer by Ann, who was learning already that the things impossible with man are possible with God. She was sitting in her chair shortly after this, between the kitchen door and the back stairway. The door having been left ajar, to her surprise a hen came in and dropped down at Ann's feet. Something said to her, "Lift it up and put it on the first step of the stair." Intuitively Ann recognised that her Father was about to meet her need. The hen went upstairs, and in her simple way Ann asked that it might not be permitted to cackle, lest Dr. Reid's daughters should hear it. (In the village at that time there was another unique character who was the laughing-stock of the boys because she permitted the hens to live in her house, and Ann did not want to be likened to old Peggy Casey). After a few minutes the hen came down very quietly and Ann reached to the door and let her out.

Then another great difficulty faced her. She had not put any weight on her foot for a long time. It was impossible for her to walk, and while she was confident that the doctor's prescription had been filled at the top of the stairs, she did not know how she was to obtain it. She prayed and felt the answer came, "Go up for it." But in her simple way she said, "Father, how can I? It is impossible." Some time before this she had learned a little refrain which she had taken as one of the motto verses of her life. It ran like this:

"Faith, mighty faith, the promise sees,
And looks to God alone,
Laughs at impossibilities
And cries, 'It shall be done'."

When she spoke of impossibilities the inward voice said, "Well, say your verse." She hesitated for some time, but at last faith conquered and she repeated the simple words. Then she received her instructions as to how she was to act. She worked her chair toward the door, and then, sitting on the first step, she raised herself with her hands, step after step, until she had reached the top. The hen had laid the egg in an old box just at the head of the stair, and she was able to reach it without getting off the top step. But how was she to get down with the egg in her hand? In her simple way - for she used to pray about all these little things in a very familiar manner - she asked for directions, and the word came, "Put it in your pocket." She then managed to descend in the same fashion, and was just safely back in her chair when Paddy, the servant, walked in. Ann prayed, "Now, Father, don't let him ask me where I got it," and in response to her simple faith he took the egg without a word and fixed it for her without making any enquiry. This is the more surprising when it is stated that he had been all though the village in his endeavour to secure eggs for Ann.

For three weeks the hen returned every day without making the slightest noise. At the end of this time the doctor one morning said she did not need any more milk and eggs, and recommended beef tea instead. Just after this one of the young ladies came in, and the hen, disturbed, came cackling downstairs. The young woman was very much startled, and said, "What, Ann, have you got hens upstairs like old Peggy Casey?" And as the hen came cackling down, the young girl shooed it out into the yard and it never returned. Afterwards when Ann was able to get out again she tried to single out this one in order to show it special kindness, but was unable to do so. When in her customary way she appealed to her Father to show her which one it was, she heard the voice speaking to her inward consciousness, and telling her, "My glory will I not give to another." For a long time Ann hesitated to speak of this incident, but her diffidence in telling of God's goodness was reproved, for she heard Him say, "I fed you just as really as I fed Elijah through the ravens, and yet you are ashamed to make it known."

Some time after her experience with the hen Ann was away from home visiting some friends in the country. She ventured to tell them how her Father had provided for her in her sickness. The lady of the house expressed her unbelief, but Ann said quietly, "Well, my Father will make you believe it before I go." And sure enough He did. Ann had not the money to take her home, and one morning as she knelt in prayer she asked her Father how much it would cost, and had just received the answer when the door opened and the lady of the house stood there. Ann said, "Oh, come in, till I see if you can count as well as my Father." She came in and reckoned up the mileage and what the fare would be, and it was exactly the same amount as that which Ann had been told. Then the woman said, "Do you think you will get it, Ann?" She replied, "To be sure I shall. I am sure of it, for the silver and the gold are my Father's, and the cattle upon a thousand hills, and I am sure He will send it to me." That morning she started out with the woman's mother to spend the day. She had only been away about half an hour when a man called and asked for the "shouting girl." The woman said, "She has just gone out for the day," and then she added in an amused way, "Do you know, she was praying this morning for money to take her back home, and she says she is sure her Father will send it." "Well," said the man, "and so am I, for I have it here in my pocket." He then told her how he had been impressed to give her the amount, and had been sent around with it. The woman was astonished, and when she saw Ann returning that evening she ran out to meet her and at once proceeded to tell her the good news. In a quiet, matter-of-fact way Ann said, "Didn't I tell you? I knew my Father would send it to me. You remember you wouldn't believe about the egg, and I told you my Father would make you believe before I left. So now this has come for you." In order to avoid the point of the remark the woman said, "Well, give me the money then, if it has come for me," but quickly Ann replied, "No. The money was sent for me, but the lesson is for you."

It must not be thought, however, that Ann's prayers were always selfish. She had a large heart for the needs of others. Every spring she used to make two barrels of soft soap - one for their own use, and always one for the poor. On one occasion she had made the one barrelful and was at the last kettleful of the second, when something seemed to go wrong and it would not thicken. The children came out to see how she was getting along, and of course, child-like, they all wanted to know what was the matter with the soap. In her familiar way Ann said, "My Father says it only needs a bone." They asked, "Well, haven't you got one?" Said she, "No, but my Father bids me wait till morning." "But suppose it should rain in the night? The water would spoil it more." But Ann quietly said, "My Father said wait till the morning, and I will wait, and cover it up now." By three o'clock the next morning Ann was up and out to see her soap. There by the side of the kettle lay a large marrow bone, from which the meat had all been taken, but which had not been boiled. With her quiet, "Thank you," Ann lifted up her heart in praise, and then picking up the axe, proceeded to break the bone and put it in the soap and in a short time it had the desired effect. The children were very anxious to see the outcome of Ann's faith. Her calm confidence in these matters had already produced an effect in the home, and they somehow expected to see Ann's prayers answered. When, in reply to their query, she said that the bone had come, "It was here by the kettle when I came out," one of the children said, "Oh, I guess a dog dropped the bone there." Like a flash Ann retorted, "I don't care if the devil brought it; my Father sent it."

As showing her interest and sympathy with others, another incident is told which was well verified at the time. The Salvation Army had opened up a station in the village and Ann became interested in them. She found on enquiry that the officers in charge were really in actual need. She asked some friends with whom she was staying if they ever took them in any food. They replied that they had on several occasions, but added, "We haven't very much to give." Ann asked the woman if she would not take them some eggs, but the response was that the hens were not laying then. Ann said, "Well, but if I ask my Father for them, will you give them to the officers?" The woman replied, "Yes, I will."

Ann went to prayer, and shortly afterwards she proceeded to the barn and gathered over a dozen eggs. The woman was amazed and wanted to know where she got them, but Ann would not satisfy her curiosity in the matter. As bearing upon this incident, it is a significant fact that this woman years afterwards sent in to the city to request Ann's prayers.

Of course, in many of these incidents one may find a natural explanation, and we are not trying to narrate these experiences with the thought that a miracle was wrought in every instance. God frequently uses natural things in order to answer the prayers of His children. Of course, some may say that the things all happened by chance, but it is certainly a most convenient chance that always appears to meet the needs of those who cry unto God.

THE STORY OF THE WELL

One of the most remarkable answers to prayer in Ann's experience was that in which she obtained water in a dry well. This incident has been told and retold scores of times, with all sorts of variations and additions. I was most careful to get the full particulars and surrounding circumstances taken down as Ann narrated it. The event occurred in the long, dry weeks of summer. During this period the well at their home was usually dry for two or three months, and the boys were compelled to haul water in barrels from the well about half a mile away. This was very hard work, and especially when they had to provide, not only for household needs, but for the stock as well. One evening at the close of the day Ann was sitting in the kitchen with the boys around her, telling them some of the remarkable ways in which her Heavenly Father had answered her prayers. When she had just concluded one of these narratives, Henry said, "Ann, why don't you ask your Father to send water in that well, and not have us boys work so hard? I was down in the well looking at it today, and it is just as dry as the floor." This was thrown out to Ann in a half-joking, half-earnest way, as though to challenge her faith. He little dreamt of the serious way that Ann would take it. When she got up into her little room that night she knelt in prayer and said, "Now, Father, you heard what Henry said tonight. If I get up in class meeting and say, 'My God shall supply all your needs accordingly to his riches in glory by Christ Jesus,' the boys won't believe I am what I profess to be if you don't send the water in the well." She then continued to plead that the water might be sent, and finally, rising from her knees, she said, "Now, Father, if I am what I profess to be, there will be water in the well in the morning." When she came down the next morning Henry was out preparing to go for the water as usual. To his surprise and great amusement he saw Ann take up the two pails and start for the well. He watched her from the kitchen window as she hooked the pail to the windlass and began to lower it. If she had done it the night before it would have gone with a bang to the bottom, but after a while there was a splash, and still down the pail went, and Ann began with difficulty to wind up the windlass again, and at last put the pail upon the well-stand full of water. She repeated this, and with both pails full of clear, sparkling water, she walked up to the house. And who could wonder that there was a little air of victory as she set down the pails and said to Harry, "Well, what do you say now?" To her surprise he simply answered, "Well, why didn't you do that long ago, and have saved us all that work?" Meditation upon that question, thrown out so thoughtlessly by this young boy, might yield some very profitable results. How often we go hungry and thirsty, suffering the lack of all sorts of needed things when a full supply might be ours! "We have not, because we ask not." Years after a friend visited the well and was told that from the time referred to the well had never been known to be dry summer or winter.

LINKING DIVINE KNOWLEDGE WITH EARTHLY NEEDS

It will be impossible for many Christians to understand the intimacy and familiarity with which Ann addressed the Divine Being. To some it will sound almost irreverent - yea, we question whether there are not those who would think it blasphemous to speak in the simple way that Ann was accustomed to do of her Heavenly Father. Further, we know there are those who would protest against bringing the thousand and one little matters of everyday life into the sphere of prayer. It was quite a common thing for Ann to go around at her daily tasks talking as familiarly to the Heavenly Father about every little thing as she would talk to any other person that might be in the home. Moreover, she sought guidance in every little detail of life.

That she received special answers, those who lived with her have no doubt. Even the children in their play would run to Ann for a solution of the little difficulties that arose. One of the boys on one occasion had lost a spade, and was dreading the wrath of his father when he should discover that the article was missing. In his distress he went to Ann and appealed to her to ask her Father about it. She at once in her simple way closed her eyes and said, "Father, where is it?" We cannot explain how she understood, or in what form these answers made themselves known to her consciousness, but she immediately made a beeline for the back of the garden, where the spade was lying hidden in the grass. This was not by any means an isolated case. The children would come to her when their toys were lost, and invariably after Ann prayed she would at once go to where the missing article was lying.

Only on one occasion did she fail to get her answer about such things, and this exception happened thus: A young minister visited the home and was out on the lawn playing croquet with the girls. Ann did not approve of this; at least she did not think it was right for the minister to be spending his time in that way. In her blunt way she asked if he could keep his mind stayed upon God while he was doing this. He replied, "Oh, yes for a little while." As the game proceeded, one of the young ladies lost a much-prized locket. However, she was quite unconcerned and said, "Oh, never mind. Ann will soon find it for me." She came in and said, "Ann, get if for me now, quick." Ann, in her usual way, went to her Father, but no answer came. She went out to look for it, but could not find it, and it was never found.

Many, many years after she had left the Reid family she came to live at our home. The boys had heard a great deal about Ann's wonderful experiences, and naturally expected to see some demonstration. They hardly liked to ask at first to ask Ann to demonstrate these things, but they used to hide things which Ann would need to use, and then watch to see how she would find them. Perhaps some article of clothing would be put in the most out-of-the-way place they could think of, and then they would watch for the time when Ann would need to use it. Being perfectly ignorant of what had occurred, she would go up to her room or walk up to a corner with her eyes closed, and in her simple way she would say, "Father, where is it?" and after standing a moment or two in silence she would turn around and go direct to the place it was hidden. We do not profess to explain this; we simply narrate what has occurred over and over again. At one place the boys hid the cat and Ann was asked where it was. She had no idea of what had been done, but in her simple way she looked up in prayer, and then made straight for the stove and opened the oven door, when the cat at once jumped out.

Of course in a Christian home such things would not occur very often to satisfy mere idle curiosity. It was not long before those who knew her felt it was too solemn a thing to be thus dealt with. However, in times of need there was never any question as to the fact of Ann's prayers being answered. On one occasion she had risen in the morning, and, as usual, had asked her Father for a verse with which to start the day. The special portion that was given to her was, "And we know that all things work together for good to them that love God." It came while they were at family prayer, and Ann said, "And we will see it before night, too. God will show it." All through the day Ann watched, but nothing unusual happened. However, when the girls returned from meeting that night Ann asked if they had had a good meeting. One of them answered, "Why, how could we when I lost all the money I had to live on next week on the way there?" Then they told how the money had been lost and they had looked for it all the evening with a lantern. Before they retired, at the family altar Ann reminded her Father of the promise of the morning, and asked that He would keep the money for her wherever it was. Early in the morning she was wakened with the instruction, "Arise and get the money that you gave Me to keep for you last night." Then came the other voice: "Nonsense! Your leg is too bad for you to get up and go." She did not obey at once and was just falling to sleep when again the voice spoke, bidding her to arise. She went out and walked down the path, not looking specially for it, but all at once she was stopped by her Father and she saw a bill lying almost hidden with the snow by the side of a small hill. She picked it up and took it across the road, where her friend, Mrs. Hughes, lived. Rapping at the door, she said, "Get up and see if this is a bill." The lady took the bill and looked at it in amazement, and said, "This is a five-dollar bill." Ann said, "Come and let us praise the Lord for this." After prayer Ann went back home, and going in, threw the bill down and said, "There; there is your money." The girls looked at it in surprise, for they had searched so long for it. Then they said, "O Ann, don't tell it in class meeting, or people will think we were so careless."

A WONDERFUL TEACHER

We know that many will have their doubts as we record God's dealings with Ann in the matter of instruction in so-called secular things. We have recorded how after attending school for some days the teacher gave up, after striving in vain in a hopeless effort to teach Ann the letters of the alphabet. We have further remarked that, at the time of her conversion, in a strange way she was enabled to read one verse from the Word of God to bring comfort and strength to her heart. Still later, at the time when she yielded absolutely to the Lord and was filled with His Spirit, was she enabled to make out a special verse that had brought light and help to her soul. Without any human intervention this process of instruction continued until Ann could read her Bible anywhere and everywhere. In the early stage it seemed almost as though, apart from the letters, she understood the words, but in her later years she was enabled to spell out the words. The most remarkable thing, however, about the whole was that Ann to the very close of life was utterly unable to read any other book. We remember on one occasion putting a paper before her and seeing her in vain trying to decipher some of the smaller words. She found it an impossible task. Finally she put her finger on one word and said, "That seems to be 'lord', but I don't think it is my Lord, as my heart doesn't burn while I see it." The writer then looked over the paper and found her finger upon the word indicated, but noticed that it was a report regarding the South African War, in which it spoke of Lord Roberts' achievements.

We do not attempt to explain at all this strange phenomenon, but we do know on the testimony of many credible witnesses that it was so. Both in public and private Ann could freely, not to say fluently, read from the Word of God, and it was marvellous the way the truth would flow forth from her lips when speaking at her Father's bidding.

While she found it utterly impossible to memorise Scripture, yet she made it so constantly her meat and drink that the Holy Spirit could bring to her remembrance just the passage suited to the occasion. A great many can testify to the aptness and point of the Scriptures that Ann would give on different occasions. It was quite a common thing for Christian people visiting the home to request

Ann to ask her Father for a verse for them, and in a wonderful way, after lifting up her eyes and her heart heavenward, Ann would give forth some passage which was evidently most suited to the special need; in fact, without knowing circumstances, she became over and over again the medium for the Divine voice either to guide, comfort or correct those who thus sought her ministry.

HEAVENLY MNEMONICS

It is sometimes difficult to understand the contradictions in a life. In the case of Ann there are those who would imagine that she had a wonderful memory, simply because she was always pouring forth Scripture verses; in fact, the Scriptures were woven into her everyday phraseology and she seemed to express herself more readily in Bible language than in any other way. To some who knew her gift in this manner it may come as a surprise to know that one of Ann's sorest trials in the early days was her lack of memory, and to the end of her life she always protested that she had no natural memory. If she desired a verse of Scripture to bear upon a certain line she would walk over to a corner of the room and with uplifted heart she would ask her Father for a suitable portion, and the word would be given her and she would tell it out, often with wonderful power and an aptness that everyone had to acknowledge.

In her early life she had a great desire to memorise Scripture verses. One day she tried for an hour to get a verse, but she found it impossible to remember it. The next day she went to a friend, who requested her to stay with the baby while she went down town. Ann took charge, and then prayed that the child might sleep during the whole time of her friend's absence so that she might once more try to learn her verse. She got a New Testament and went over and over the same verse again, but without success. Finally it seemed as though the voice spoke to her and asked, "Ann, what is the matter with you?" Ann replied, "Well, I never saw the like of me. I spell and spell, but can't remember a word," and she broke out crying. Then the voice spake again, "Well, I thought Christ was a satisfying portion - all in all to you?" Ann replied, "Well, Father, I would like to remember these verses." Her Father said, "What do you want to get that message for?" Ann replied, "Well, the class leader always quotes it in his prayer, and I like it." The special verse she was trying to memorise was, "Whatsoever ye desire, when ye pray believe that ye receive it and ye shall have it." The reply came back again, "Did you ever see a mother send a child on an errand and observe that the child forgot it before it got half way to its destination? Well, you would be just the same. But I will give it to you just when I want you to have it, and then you won't have time to forget."

This seemed to satisfy Ann in a measure, but she then in a persistent way said, "Won't you teach me the little things on the doors?" She could never tell the number of a house. The voice replied, "Why do you want to be able to read them?" She said, "So that I could go around by myself." Then came the answer, "No, for then you would go to places where they do not want you and where I did not send you. I will always take you myself or send a pilot." Ann was so ignorant that she did not know the meaning of this last word, but the next morning a woman came for her to go and pray with her mother, who was dying, and she was instructed to go with this pilot, and then Ann understood.

I shall never forget my own experience with Ann in this line. She had been invited by my parents to come and live with us altogether, and I was deputed to return with Ann to the city while she collected her belongings. I was a perfect stranger in the city and in consequence was of no service in finding the location of places. She had left her things here and there all over, and she could neither tell the names of the persons or streets nor the numbers of the houses. Here and there she would recall possibly a name, and on some occasions would remember the street. We set out one morning to visit the places where she had left different articles of clothing. I carried her valise. She could not tell me where she was going first, but we would walk along the street, and suddenly Ann would stop and ask her Father which way to turn. I was not used to praying on street corners, and frankly confess that I felt at times somewhat ashamed to be in Ann's company. To find the first house we at last went into a store. Ann had the name of the person given to her, but did not know where she lived. The storekeeper was busy, but said that she had moved and was living on such and such a street, and gave the number. Seeing that I was a stranger, he said he would write down the street and number for us. As he turned around for a pencil, Ann said, "Father, don't let him find it." After looking for some time, he came back and said, "Well, that is strange. I had a pencil here just a little while ago, and I can't find it. I guess I will put on my hat and go out with you and show you the place." This simplified matters in the first call.

At the next place Ann could not remember the name of the individual, and evidently did not know the house. Several times as we walked on she said, "That looks like the house," but was directed to go past. Finally she stopped and said, "My Father says this is the house." I said, "Well, Ann, you can go up and see; I am not going." It seemed to me too ridiculous a thing to ring the doorbell and meet people without knowing who you wanted to see or where they lived. With perfect confidence Ann went up and rang the bell, and when the people came, turned around in a kind of triumphant way and beckoned for me to come up. This kind of experience was repeated over and over again that day. It was at first very mortifying to me, and then, to conclude matters, Ann wanted me to go that night to the Salvation Army with her. I went along, and when the opportunity was given for testimony Ann jumped up and in a joyful way began to praise her Father for the way He had led her that day and guided her aright, and then turning to me and directing all attention upon me, she said, "She was afraid to trust my Father. She wouldn't believe that the Lord could guide me to the right houses," and then concluded by turning and saying to me, "Now, you get up and speak." As far as my own feelings were concerned, the day did not end triumphantly, but I certainly had learned that Ann had a strange power and that she had such intimate guidance as I had never seen exhibited in anyone before.

PROVIDENTIAL PROTECTION

In her long career Ann had quite a number of narrow escapes, and there were several occasions on which it seemed as though the powers of evil had designed either to destroy her life or rob her of virtue. On one occasion Ann was out in the bush gathering some wood, as she did not care to trouble anyone else to do it. In a very lonely part a man suddenly appeared, and after watching her, asked why she was gathering wood, and why her husband did not do that kind of work for her. Innocently Ann answered, "I have no husband. I am joined to the Lord." Looking around in every direction, he asked, "How far is it to the nearest house?" "Oh," Ann said, "it is a good way off." Then, as though restrained, he said, "Well, if you come down tomorrow I will bring a big load of wood here, but don't come till after dark." Quite innocently Ann promised that she would come for it. That night she received a warning dream, in which the evil intentions of the man were revealed and Ann was saved from what was evidently a snare prepared for her. Many years afterward, while visiting in the lower section of the city, she was asked by a friend to call at a certain house which was notorious as a den of vice. When Ann entered the door she recognised the man who kept the place the very one who had met her in the bush years ago, and one of the women that were with him immediately recognised Ann. The old lady at once knelt down in that sinful place and prayed for them. As she confessed, she was very glad to get out of it once more.

On another occasion Ann was alone in the house. She had finished her churning on this particular morning, and carried the buttermilk downstairs, but instead of taking it through into the milk cellar, she put it just at the foot of the steps, finding, as her custom was, to clean out the dairy first. Ann, in her usual way, was talking to her Father, and said she was coming back to finish this work later on. After dinner, when she was left alone, she proceeded to wash up the dishes, and then, noticing a small hole in the carpet, she said, "I will mend this, Father, before I go down in the cellar to clean." While thus engaged a man entered their lane and came toward the house. Ann paid little heed to him, but proceeded with her work. She said that he turned aside into the hedge for a little while, and when he came out had his arm in a sling. While she was working on the carpet he suddenly appeared in the doorway and asked for help. Ann said, "I have nothing." "Where are the girls?" he queried. Ann said, "They are gone out for the afternoon and won't be back till evening." "Where's the men?" "Back in the bush," she said. "How far away is that?" He continued. "About half a mile," Ann said. Satisfied that there was no one around, he asked her if she could get him a drink of buttermilk, knowing that she would have to go into the cellar for it. Ann said, "Yes, sir,

I can," and at once proceeded down the steps. Her Father said, "Be quick," and then Ann began to be afraid. She ran with all her might to the foot of the stairs and dipped into the crock for a drink and rushed up again, but not until the man had made his way and stood at the top of the steps. However, her sudden return with the can in her hand seemed so to surprise him that he backed away from the cellarway and then took the milk. After he had taken a drink Ann again kneeled down to finish mending the hole. The man sat down and asked Ann if she would mend a small tear in his trousers. The man said he had torn it in going into the hedge to tie up his arm in a sling. She did not know what to do and so in order to get time she proceeded with the thread and needle to carry out his wish, praying all the while that the Lord would take care of her. She was convinced that the man intended robbery. Ere she had finished with her needle and thread, to her great relief she heard the windlass creaking at the well, and at once jumped up and said, "Oh, there is Mr. Reid now, sir." But the man evidently did not want to meet him and slunk away, trembling, Ann said, as though he had the palsy. She felt that God had delivered her.

Two or three days after this, just about the same time in the afternoon, she was occupied outside in the cook house when she noticed a queer looking old woman coming up the avenue to the house. Her strange appearance struck Ann at once as being very peculiar. She said, "Who is it, Father?" Instantly her answer came, "Don't you remember the man who was here the other day?" "Yes,

Father, is it him?" "Yes it is," came the answer. This time he walked up and said, "I want to see the boss." Although there was not another soul on the farm, Ann said, "Just step in, ma'am, and I will call him." Ann at once ran toward the well, calling at the top of her voice, "Mr. Reid! Mr. Reid!" When the old woman heard her shouting she turned and hobbled away, saying, "Never mind." Ann was sorely tried over this, as it was a question to her mind whether she had not told a lie when she acted in this manner, knowing that Mr. Reid was not around. However, she was somewhat consoled in the remembrance that the first time the man came she had told him the truth, even although her life was in danger.

Another incident occurred years after, when the Reid family had grown up and Ann was living in the little cottage which they had bought for her ere they gave up the old homestead.

When the two girls left home they decided to go out to the far Western States, then just being opened up, and when they had left they placed all their goods to be stored in Ann's little cottage. Some of the things were valuable, but they had perfect confidence in Ann's care and integrity. However, it was at this time that a neighbour began to covet possession of these things. The two girls had expected to return home within a year, but instead of that years went by and they were still living in the Western States. The neighbour woman before referred to was one of disreputable character, and while she professed friendship for Ann, yet she did her utmost to undermine her. On one occasion when Ann was very sick she came in and proffered her services, but Ann had no confidence whatever in the woman, and tried to decline. However, she persistently pressed herself in upon her. Ann suffered greatly from dropsy and heart trouble, and this woman, evidently having designs upon the valuables that she knew were in Ann's care, came in one day and insisted on Ann drinking a cup of tea. Ann had been warned by her Father not to receive anything from her, and when she came in she refused to take it, but the woman fairly glared at Ann and insisted, and under the pressure through fear Ann finally took the cup and drank it. The woman then went out. Ann was sorely tried because she felt that she had gone contrary to the revealed will of her Father, and Satan said, "Now He won't hear your prayer." But in an instant Ann was crying out, "Father, forgive me, forgive me. You know I love you better than anything else in the world. But you know I was afraid. Now, Father, like as a father pitieth his children, pity me. You know my frame and you remember that I am but dust." Instantly she received the assurance of forgiveness, and to her mind was brought at once very vividly the incident in the life of Paul, where he was bitten by the viper, and she received the assurance that God would take care of her, even though poisoned. In a little while she became very, very sick, and vomited incessantly for a long time. She felt that this saved her life. The woman tried to get the care of Ann again, time after time, but by very special providences her efforts along this line were blocked and her purposes frustrated.

Ann firmly believed that in the above instance she had received the fulfilment of the Scripture promise, "If they drink any deadly thing it shall not hurt them."

A GODLESS BROTHER

Some years after Ann's arrival in this country, Canada, hearing that her only brother was living a very sinful life, she became concerned about him, and thinking that he would do better in the New World, she sent for him. For a while it seemed as though there was a little change, and he professed to get converted, but there was no depth to it, and shortly after he plunged more deeply into sin than ever. He hated to have Ann enter the home, and many a time in a drunken fit he had threatened her life. Ann was never afraid of him, however. Once after she had rebuked him for his sinful life, he picked up a chair and threatened to kill her with it. Ann looked at him as bold as a lion, and said, "If the devil has the chair, my Father has the guiding of it, and indeed you will not do it." Ann says he dropped the chair with force enough to have broken it. It was a great grief to Ann to see the example which he set to his little girl. He used to send her to the saloon for his drink. Ann felt this so keenly that after rebuking him for it she made it a special matter of prayer, and getting a glimpse of the life of sin that seemed inevitable for the little girl under such surroundings, she cried out to God to save her and to take her away from the evil which was to come. She received assurance that this would be granted, and boldly told her brother that it was the last time that he would ever be permitted to send her for his liquor. This enraged him, but did not alter the decree. For a few days the child happened to be otherwise occupied when the hour came to go for the liquor, and then she took sick. As she grew worse they became uneasy and appealed to Ann to pray for the child's recovery. But she told them plainly that she knew her Father was going to take the child away to deliver her from such a wicked home. A few days after this she fell asleep, leaving behind a clear testimony of her faith in the Lord Jesus.

Ann did not cease to visit this brother, even when some miles intervened between them. On one occasion she was staying with a friend, when one morning she received word from her Father that she was to go to see her brother James that day. Ann replied, "Sure, Father, I cannot go; it is five miles, and I could not walk." The reply came, "You do as I tell you. The earth is the Lord's and the fullness thereof. The silver and the gold are His, and the cattle upon a thousand hills." Ann saw it in a minute and said, "The horses, too, Father." She went on with her work. Just when she had got the dinner ready her Father said, "Now, is the time to go." Turning to one of the girls, Ann told her that she must go. They urged her to stay and take her dinner, but Ann insisted that her Father had said, "Now is the time." They said, "Very well, you can do a little errand for us on your way. Just call in and tell Mrs. ___ to send over two pounds of butter." Ann hurried off and away in the distance behind she saw coming over the hill a gray horse. Her Father said, "That is the horse that is to take you." She hurried down the road to get the errand done first. Just before she entered the house she saw the horse stop at the tavern. She at once said, "Sure, Father, that cannot be the one, or it would not stop there." But the answer came, "Yes, that is the horse to take you." When she came out of the house another rig overtook her and she accepted the invitation for a ride, but found the man was only going two miles. After a little while the gray horse overtook them and Ann said to the man who was driving her. "There, that is the horse that my Father said was to take me. Ask the man how far he is going." In reply to enquiry he said he was just going two miles, but Ann was not satisfied with the answer, and insisted that he ask again. The next time he replied that he was going five miles, and right along the road in which Ann desired to go. The man asked him if he would give Ann a ride, as she wanted to go that far. He answered, "I don't take women with me." Ann spoke up then and said, "My Father said that He sent that horse for me." The priest - for such he was - said, "What do you mean? Who is your father?" She replied, "My Heavenly Father. " He then said, "Well, jump in." So Ann got in, and all the way along she talked to the priest about her Father and His wonderful Word. That some impression was made can be judged by the fact that, although the priest was turning off some little way before reaching Ann's destination, he very kindly undertook to drive her wherever she wanted to go. Ann thanked him, but got out and walked the rest of the way, praising God for the provision made for her.

She reached the home of her brother, and it seemed as though, while her own brother constantly rejected her message, that God intended her to minister to his wife, for it was not long before this poor woman was wonderfully converted, and the change was just as real and deep as in the life of Ann herself. She was led into an experience of very close intimacy with God, and although living in a drunkard's home she had wonderful answers to her prayers and led a life that commended the Gospel which she proclaimed.

A FAITHFUL SERVANT

It has been written, "He that is faithful in that which is least shall be made ruler of much," and it is a general principle that those who are untrue in the so-called secular matters of life can never be made powerful in the spiritual realm. Ann kept her covenant with the Reid family and stayed with them until, first Mrs. Reid and then later the old doctor, had passed away, nor did her task end then; she continued to keep house for the family that was left until they grew up and her services were required no longer. Even then she constantly followed them with her prayers. Two of the boys left the old homestead determined to seek their fortunes in the South, and took up residence in New Orleans. A cousin accompanied them on this journey. They had not long resided there when a terrible plague of yellow fever visited the city. People died by hundreds and thousands and were carted away to the outskirts of the city without any ceremony whatever. For two weeks at this period, without knowing what was occurring, Ann had a great burden of prayer, and used to go daily to her friend, Mrs. Hughes, and together they interceded on behalf of the two absent boys. During this time Ann had a vision one night that Joshua, the youngest, had died. So certain was she of this that the next morning she visited Mrs. Hughes and told her that she knew Joshua was dead, and that she could no longer pray for him. This friend tried to persuade Ann that it was the constant thought and care for the boys and her undue anxiety that caused her to think thus. But Ann was persistent in stating that her Father had given her the dream, and that it must be so. The cousin kept in correspondence with the two girls who were at home with Ann. He reported that both of the boys had fever, but it was not until six weeks after, when Henry, the other brother, had fully recovered from the fever, that he sent home word that Joshua had died, and when the date became known it was found that it was on the very night of Ann's dream.

When the family needed Ann's services no longer they very kindly fitted up for her a little cottage in the village and made her as comfortable as possible, the boys assuring her that as long as they lived she should never want. However, man's proposals are often very different from that which is brought to pass. It was not long before all the boys were dead and Ann was thrown entirely upon the loving care of her Heavenly Father.

Ann continued to reside in her little cottage for some years, and then for a time returned to the home of a member of the Reid family, but later on accepted an invitation to come and spend a little time with her old friend, Mrs. Hughes, who had moved to the City of Toronto. This temporary arrangement continued for some years, and Toronto became her home. There is no doubt that God's providence was in this, leading Ann into a wider sphere of usefulness and blessing, for her testimony was given in many of the city churches, and her influence was felt far and wide.

CORRECTING THE CATHOLIC BISHOP

She was not posing as a new Reformer, although even Luther before the Diet of Worms did not stand more fearlessly for the truth than this little Irish woman would when occasion demanded. It is true she was too insignificant a Protestant to cause Rome to tremble, but on the other hand, all the Cardinals and Prelates in the world could not have intimidated this humble saint, or have silenced her tongue when she was moved to speak. Ann had been detained through stress of weather with a Catholic friend one Saturday night. This good lady pressed her on Sunday morning to accompany her to the Cathedral. In response to the invitation, Ann decided that she would go. The friend took her into one of the front seats, and together they sat while the (to Ann) strange introductory services and ceremonial proceeded. After this came a sermon by the Bishop. Unfortunately, on this occasion his address was taken up with a contrast between Roman Catholicism and the Protestant churches, and he proceeded to take up the various denominations one by one for consideration. Ann's knowledge of Church history was certainly very limited, and relative claims to antiquity were meaningless to her, as decades, centuries or ages were all alike to her mind. Consequently she understood very little of what was being said until the priest came to the Methodists. Then Ann was all alive at once with interest, as she was now on familiar ground. He commenced by saying that the Methodists were a little, upstart people, founded by a cobbler and in existence but a short time. This was too much for Ann, who immediately stood up and said, "That's not so," and proceeded to explain that they had been in existence for some considerable period, for she had known them for full forty years. Her good friend was mortified and terribly dismayed, and at once tired to pull Ann to her seat. However, Ann was not to be so easily swerved from her position. Turning to her friend, she said, "Stop plucking me; I am not a goose," and she proceeded to tell the people what Methodists were. However, two young priests came toward her, and one of them very respectfully said, "Madam, it is wrong for you to speak here. The Scriptures say that women must keep silence in the churches, and if they wish to know anything they must ask their husbands at home." To this remonstrance Ann replied, "I have no husband. I am joined to the Lord, so I will ask Him here," and she at once proceeded to pray. After this she quietly sat in her seat during the rest of the service. The people were so indignant that anyone would dare to contradict their Bishop that they were angry enough to have torn her to pieces at the close, but her friend and some others who knew her came forward and pleaded her cause, and Ann was allowed to go in peace.

Ann was just as bold, however, in her own church. On one occasion they were having a union class meeting at Thornhill, when nearly the whole of the testimonies were simply the confession of heart wanderings and deviations from the will of God, and the whole atmosphere was more like a Jewish wailing place than an old-time Methodist class meeting. Finally Ann could stand it no longer. She jumped to her feet and marched to the front, and then facing the crowd, she said, "Would to God you'd have done with your heart wanderings and your devotions. You give my Father's table a bad name. Who, after hearing you this morning, would want to come? You keep people away from the Lord," and then she told them the secret of a joyful Christian life.

PRAYER FOR HEALING

It is not to be wondered at that the remarkable answers that Ann received to her prayers should have led people in different distresses to appeal to Ann for help, and it was not at all an uncommon thing for the sick to ask for Ann's prayers. There are many records of wonderful answers along this line.

While assisting in special services in Brooklyn, she called on a Mrs. R. who was very low with typhoid fever. As an aggravating symptom, the poor patient found it utterly impossible to obtain sleep. Ann knelt by the bedside in her simple way and asked her Heavenly Father to give at least two hours of quiet sleep. As soon as her petition was ended she went out confidently into the adjoining room and asked the members of the family to keep very quiet, stating that she had asked her Father to give two hours' sleep, and added, "I know He will." The patient went right off and for four hours had quiet, restful sleep, and from that point health began to return.

It must not be thought, however, that Ann would pray indiscriminately according to the requests of the people. She had to learn early that it was impossible to persistently press for answers to prayer that when granted would only prove a hindrance and a curse. On one occasion a husband came to Ann in great distress and said the doctor had given up on his wife, and that it was impossible for her to live. Piteously he appealed to Ann to pray for her life to be spared to her family. He said, "I know your faith will bring her back." Ann was entreated and went to her Father in a presumptuous way and said, "If I am what I profess, I will have her life." She even used stronger expressions which we do not care to repeat. The woman was restored immediately and lived for years a life that dishonoured her Lord an brought discredit on the cause of Christ. Ann humbly confessed the rashness of her prayer.

Some might take exception to the subjects that came within the range of Ann's petitions. The writer well remembers the coming of Ann to her home. After she had been there a short time my youngest brother said to Ann, "We haven't seen any of the wonderful things that they tell about done around here since you came." A few days after this one of the cows was taken very sick and Ann heard the men say that she could not get better and must be shot. Ann went out to the pasture field and looked at the cow, and just decided that it was very, very sick, when the Lord said, "Now, here is your chance." Ann said, "Chance for what?" The reply came, "To show them that My power is unchanged." Ann had another look and then decided it was indeed a good chance, but her faith was not staggered by the appearance of things, and she confidently said, "Well, Father, I will take it then by faith," although, Gideon-like, she asked for two or three signs before she was entirely satisfied and could go back and meet my younger brother with the assurance that she knew the cow would soon be well. My brother clapped his hands at the statement, and said, "Oh good! It will get better now." In his boyish way he used to sometimes like to test Ann's faith afterward. When he went back for the cows that night he came home quiet disappointed and said, "Ann, it is no better." But this did not disturb Ann's confidence, and shortly after the cow was perfectly restored.

THE HABIT OF PRAYER

We have referred so often to the manner in which Ann would go around in constant conversation and fellowship with God, that some might be inclined to think that this was the beginning and end of her prayer life. However, she from the commencement of the life of victory found it absolutely essential to get alone with God, to enter the closet, to close the door, that she might pray to her Father in secret. A Salvation Army officer who had heard Ann testify, and who was evidently deeply impressed, had a great desire to know whether her private life was in accord with her public utterances. Providentially at a special meeting she was sent for the night to the same home at which Ann was staying, and they were put in the same room to sleep.

The officer tells how, long after they had got into bed, Ann lay quietly communing with her Father, ejaculating praise from time to time, until nearly midnight. About five o'clock in the morning she awoke, in her usual way, praising God.

The dawn had not yet broken, and experiencing some difficulty in finding her clothing, she just asked her Father where the articles were, and at once went to the place and in her simple way said, "Thank you, Father." Then she poured water into the wash basin and began to wash.

For many years, even to the close of her life, she made it a daily custom to take a complete cold sponge bath. Just as she was preparing for this she suddenly stopped, and addressing God, she said, "What is that you say, Father?" Then in a moment she burst out with the exclamation, "Yes, that is it. Thank you, Father." And then with rapture she repeated the following verses: "Then will I sprinkle clean water upon you, and ye shall be clean; from all your filthiness, and from all your idols will I cleanse you. A new heart also will I give you, and a new spirit will I put within you, and I will take away the stoney heart out of your flesh, and I will give you an heart of flesh, and I will put My spirit within you and cause you to walk in My statutes, and ye shall keep My judgments and do them." After this she completed her toilet and then knelt in quiet prayer for at least an hour. The officer needed no further demonstration of the secret of Ann's power.

When she came to stay with us, the boys built a little prayer house for her in the midst of a little grove of cedar trees, near the back of the farm. Every day Ann used to repair for at least two hours to this quiet spot and pour out her soul to God in earnest petition. No one can measure the blessing that came down upon the lives of those for whom her petitions were uttered. Frequently she used to take my little brother back with her, and he sometimes served as an incentive to Ann's prayers. On one occasion Ann asked him where his oldest brother was, and was informed that he had gone with a number of other men to a ploughing-bee to assist one of the neighbours who had been sick all winter, and then closed his remarks by saying, "But it is a pity they will all have to come home," as it was then threatening a regular downpour of rain. Ann expressed her regret at this, and he said, "Why, Ann, couldn't you ask your Father to stop the rain?" and in his boyish way quoted her favourite verse, "Faith, mighty faith, the promise sees."

Ann at once made this matter of prayer and received assurance of her answer, and with strong faith asserted that there would be no rainfall that day. The clouds continued to gather and things looked blacker than ever, and George asserted that it was bound to come. But Ann was unmoved, and the men were permitted to finish their day's work without any hindrance from the rain.

OF LIKE PASSIONS WITH US

If we were to close this narrative and record of an unblemished career of over fifty years, many would think that we were following the custom of hero worshippers, and either with biased judgment or by suppression of facts were creating an ideal rather than recording the actual.

It is with the consciousness that we shall make the lesson of this life more effective thereby, that we venture to insert a few incidents that magnify grace by conclusively proving that the subject of this biography was throughout "a woman of like passions with us."

The Scripture injunction, "Walk in the Spirit," calls for voluntary action, and the exercise of the human will. It is equally possible to "walk after the flesh." Between these two principles, these two "walks," the believer is ever making choice, and to the end of life the will has power to yield to the one or the other. The triumphant Christian life calls for the constant exercise of faith, and union and communion with the Lord. It is written, "He that abidieth in Him sinneth not." The whole secret of Ann's victorious life was in this "abiding". While she stayed in the secret place of the Most High there was a wonderful Christlikeless, but immediately her walk of faith ceased there was every manifestation of the old nature apparent.

Mrs. Hughes, with whom Ann lived for many years, narrates two little incidents that illustrate this contrast very vividly. On one occasion Ann was attending a general rally of the Methodists of Toronto, who gathered in the Metropolitan Church for a great love-feast, to be followed by a fellowship meeting. Old Dr. Carroll was in the chair. When the opportunity for testimony was given it was not long before Ann was on her feet. The chairman did not know her, and after she had spoken at some length he very courteously reminded her that there were others who were entitled to some time as well as herself. Very sweetly Ann replied, "Yes, that is so; the time is my Father's," and in a very nice way she concluded her remarks and sat down. Before the meeting concluded someone informed Dr. Carroll as to who the old lady was, and he at once felt grieved that he had asked her to stop. At the conclusion of the service he made his way back to where Ann was standing, and very humbly expressed his regret that he had asked her to cease, and said he hoped she would not be offended. Ann at once said, "Oh, no," and then lifting up her eyes, she said, "Father, what do you say about it?" At once the answer came and Ann gave it forth from the Scripture, "Great peace have they that love thy law, and nothing shall *offend* them."

In contrast to this, the same friend accompanied Ann to a meeting in Wesley Church, at which, as soon as the opportunity occurred, Ann rose to speak for the Master. As she proceeded, one of the good brethren at the back, evidently impressed and blessed by what she was saying, began to respond. From previous experiences Ann was probably somewhat sensitive, and failing to catch what this good brother said, concluded that he was calling for her to sit down. In a moment she turned around and quite sharply said, "I will not sit down till my Father wants me to." The friend who narrates this said that on her way to the meeting Ann seemed to be just running over with the joy of the Lord, and her face fairly shone as on the street car she spoke to first one and another of the Lord Jesus. Nor had this radiance left her as she rose to speak on this occasion. "But," said this friend, "immediately after her sharp retort there was a change, and after saying a few more things Ann sat down." On the way home her good friend undertook to remonstrate with her and told her the enemy must have got hold of her ear at least in that meeting. She informed Ann that the person that she had spoken back to was simply saying, "Praise the Lord!" Ann said she thought she heard him say, "sit down." But on further explanation she became very much ashamed and humbled over her whole attitude in this matter. We simply narrate this here for the purpose of showing that apart from grace and the keeping power of the Holy Spirit, Ann was as liable to be surprised and defeated by the great Adversary as others would be.

There were several occasions on which, during the years that we knew her quite intimately, further evidences of this fact were given. As best illustrating this, we narrate one little incident that happened toward the close of her life. Ann had been invited by a friend to a city some distance from Toronto, and during her stay in the home of this gentleman, he had become greatly drawn to her, and urged her to spend the remainder of her life in his comfortable home. Through his great kindness Ann had been thrown off her guard and soon became quite infatuated with the peculiar tenets which this man held in regard to the Church as the Bride of Christ. For some three or four years previous Ann had derived great comfort from the truth of the Second Coming of Christ, and looked forward with joy to the time when He should return for His Church, and when all the saints should be "forever with the Lord."

Now, however, she was led off from the plain statements of Scripture, and by degrees the company of those who were to be caught up at the Lord's coming had been restricted and restricted until, standing on the basis practically of human righteousness, there were very few who could be included in the number of those who would rise to meet the Lord in the air at His coming. This friend and Ann were to be amongst the number. So extreme had she become in her view that for the time she seemed to have lost sight of the fundamental basis of grace. Moreover, she became so greatly occupied with this man that she began to apply to him verses of Scripture that could be only rightly applied to the Lord Jesus Himself.

Just at this time my husband was invited to preach in the church to which this gentleman belonged, and was to be entertained at his home. After the sermon Ann rose, and pointing to this man, used the words, "This is my beloved Son; hear ye Him," and directed the people to regard him as one who should be listened to in a peculiar way because of this, and stated that the Church could not be blessed unless they heeded his teaching. She spoke for some time. After the service my husband went home with them, and at the dinner table remarked that he had almost decided to sing Ann down in the meeting when she made such wrong application of Scripture, and demurred at the application of such a verse to any mere man. At this both parties reproved became quite indignant, and Ann gave good evidences of possessing some of the warmth of feeling over which she had wept and prayed so much during her early Christian life. After concluding his Sunday services, my husband decided to leave for home by the early train at five o'clock the next morning. Just before departing he heard Ann's knock at the door, and on opening it Ann stood outside saying, "My Father tells me that I am to go with you." He was very much surprised at this, as she had told him the day before that she was going to stay in this home the rest of her life. He said to her that it would be impossible for him to wait while she got ready, as it was a long walk to the depot, and he had only just time to hurry on and catch the train. She insisted, however, that her Father told her that she was to go with him. He always says that he wished he had heeded her direction, but he hurried off to catch the train. After reaching the depot he had to wait for fully an hour ere the train came, it was so late that morning.

Little more than a week had elapsed after this when Ann was sent back to her old home in Toronto under the care of a friend, she having become utterly irresponsible, and for some months her reason was beclouded and she was under the constant care of loving fiends. Whether

her weakening mental condition was the cause of her deflection from the truth, or whether a compassionate heavenly Father took this method of delivering her from a subtle delusion, it is impossible to tell. During this period she was in no way responsible for her actions.

Many friends who had known her for so long deeply felt her condition, and it was thought it would be deplorable, after all the years of her testimony, that her life should go out in that manner. Much prayer was offered up on her behalf, and after some few months the cloud lifted and she regained her wonted mental vigour and spiritual balance, and her remaining years were spent with a clear sky, and declined only, like the orb of day, to a glorious sunset.

TESTIMONY OF MINISTERS

The Rev. E. B. Ryckman, a Methodist minister at that time resident in Almonte, on seeing the obituary notice of Ann's death in one of the papers, wrote as follows to the Montreal "Witness": "Just fifty years ago now I was sent to my first station in the Toronto district. My home was at Thornhill, which was also the home of the family of Dr. Reid, in which Ann was a servant, and in a sense mistress and mother, too, for both Dr. and Mrs. Reid had passed away, and the devoted Ann had the young people under her care. I soon discovered that I had in my charge a person and a Christian of very remarkable attainments. During the fifty years of my ministry the word 'consecration' has never been interpreted to me so fully by any other as by Ann. All that is meant by the phrases, 'walking with God' and 'talking with God,' was illustrated more visibly, practically and constantly by her than by any other than I have known. One could not talk with her without talking about Christ or some interest of His Kingdom. Without the least appearance of assumption, she always controlled the conversation. She was accustomed to spake of the Almighty as was Job, and to hear Him speak to her in turn. For instance, one day I went into the Reid home, and of course the subject of religion in some interesting phase of it was up at once between Ann and myself. In the course of conversation, she spoke of her temptations. I said, as if in surprise, "Why, Ann, how is it that you are tempted?" She replied, "O, I understand it. I told the Lord about it and He said, 'Why, Ann, you are all the time trying to tear down Satan's kingdom, and of course he will not let you alone.'" He then records some incidents already referred to in this narrative and goes on to state: "The most remarkable thing about his woman was her knowledge of Scripture and the use she made of it in prayer, in the relation of Christian experience and in ordinary conversation. Generations of Methodist preachers stationed during the past sixty years on Yonge Street circuit have in turn stood astonished at Ann's familiarity with the Bible. All her wants and wishes, her joys and sorrows, indeed, all her thoughts, seemed to be such as could be most easily and fitly expressed in Scripture language. I never heard her equal even in the pulpit. Ann made the very highest profession. She affirmed that she was sanctified wholly, and that the blood of Jesus Christ cleansed her from all unrighteousness, and I never knew saint or sinner who knew her that would hint that either her conduct or her character was out of harmony with her profession, and best of all, those who knew her most intimately and the family she served, gave her most readily all credit for sincerity and consistency."

Rev. John Salmon, in writing a few reminiscences of this remarkable life, opens with the statement, "The memory of the just is blessed," Proverbs 10:7. "This was the verse impressed on my mind as I thought of our departed friend and sister in the Lord, Ann Preston, familiarly known by the very suggestive name, 'Holy Ann,' or as the Catholics would say, 'Saint Ann' - for she was a saint in the truest sense of that word.

"The memory of her prayer life has often been a benediction to me; so intimate was she with God that when one heard her pray there came a feeling of nearness to the Author of our very being, reminding us of what Moses said when he asked the question, "What nation is there so great who hath God so nigh unto them as the Lord our God is in all things that we call upon Him for?" - Deut. 4:7. I have often heard Ann, when speaking in public, quote a passage of Scripture that was brought to her mind in the following way: The passage or verse she wanted seemed not to be in her memory just at the time she wished to give it out. She would stop and say aloud, "Father, give me that verse," and the next instant would exclaim, "I have got it," and then she would repeat it verbatim, so that a person could tell at once that our sister was living in constant communion with God. Like Enoch of old, she walked with God. I remember on one occasion at a Salvation Army camp meeting, a number of us were on the platform when Ann was speaking out of the fullness of her heart. I happened to turn around to my next neighbour, the honoured and lamented William Gooderham, and I saw great tears rolling down his cheeks as that dear woman poured forth her torrents of living truth from a heart overflowing with love and praise to our God. I cannot at this time recall her words, but they were words of wonderful power sent forth by the Holy Spirit which indwelt that feeble body of clay which was lighted up by the life Divine so that her face used to shine with joy and gladness. Ann was a genial companion in her home life. Her conversation usually took the form of her experience of the Lord's kindness to her under different circumstances. She had no hesitation in saying, "My Father tells me this," and "He told me that." We might be disposed to speak as follows: Something seems to say, do this, or do that. Aye! That Something or Someone. We are afraid to say, "My Father told me." Such forms of speech show how little we know of real communion with God. Communion is the highest form of intercourse; it implies that not only do we talk to God, but that He also speaks to us. When the Lord would destroy the cities of the plain, as described in Genesis 18:17-33, He said, "Shall I hide from Abraham that which I do?" Then there begins a conversation between the Lord and Abraham, and after earnest pleading on the part of Abraham that the city should be spared, even if only ten righteous men were found in it, the Lord replied, "I will not destroy it for the ten's sake." Then follows the significant statement, "And the Lord went His way as soon as He had left communing with Abraham, and Abraham returned to his place." Communion consisted thus in the Lord talking to Abraham and Abraham talking to God. Our beloved sister Ann knew what it was thus to hold converse. Is that not what is meant when the Lord Jesus says, "My sheep here My voice and I know them, and they follow Me" ? Ours is the privilege to speak to the Master and to have the Master speak to us. Solomon prayed for a hearing heart (marginal reading), a heart to hear God's voice.

"On one occasion I was taking our sister Ann to spend a few weeks in a home near Whitby. During the passage on the train there sat behind us a Catholic priest, who became very much interested in the conversation going on between Ann and myself. I drew her out in regard to the dealings of the Lord with her answer to prayer. By and by the priest put several questions to her, which were usually answered in Scripture language. He looked at her with wonder and a certain amount of admiration, as much as to say, "Here is an uneducated old Irishwoman who evidently knows more about vital godliness than I do. What does it all mean?" He was evidently much impressed with her conversation, and who can tell what the result might be?"

Ann was always ready, in season and out of season, to give a reason for the hope that was in her. On the street car or train, in the home or on the street, she was quick to grasp the opportunity, without fear, to speak for her Lord.

Pastor Salmon continues as follows: "On one occasion Dr. Zimmerman and I were out making pastoral calls, when we went into a house and learned that our sister Ann was very sick in bed. We were ushered into a room and found she had been praying to God to send us to see her.

As we waited upon God in prayer, Ann poured out her heart something like this: "Father, sure the devil told me that my two brothers would not come to see me, as they did not know I was sick, and that I could not write to tell them how ill I was. But, Father, you told me I could telegraph them by way of the Throne of Grace. So I just telegraphed to You and now You have sent the message to them, and here they are. Glory to God!" We were filled with holy joy and laughter, and could do nothing but praise God from the bottom of our hearts. God graciously answered prayer, and Ann was immediately restored to health and testified afterward to having been raised up from a sick bed in answer to the prayer of faith given to us on that memorable visit."

We could give testimony of many other ministers, did space permit. At her funeral almost every evangelical denomination was represented, and minister after minister rose to bear witness to the wonderful influence of the life that had just closed. Ann did not hesitate to exhort, rebuke or reprove ministers when she felt they were not true to the Word of God or to the light given to them, and more than one was led to greater faithfulness to their ministry through the faithful testimony of this humble saint.

The well-known Bible teacher, Mr. W. R. Newell, gives the following testimony concerning the way in which Ann would obtain knowledge concerning individual lives in communion with her Heavenly Father. He writes:

"Several winters ago I was holding meetings in Toronto, and was staying with my wife at the China Inland Mission Home.

"One day I suggested we go to visit 'Holy Ann', whom I had met and with whose life and testimony I was profoundly impressed.

"We had an excellent talk with her. She seemed on fire with the Word of God, being occupied with nothing else. She would bring up passage after passage with a kind of holy triumph that was most refreshing.

"In the midst of her conversation she suddenly turned to my wife and said, "Many are the afflictions of the right-eous, but the Lord delivereth them out of them all. I think you will be sick. There will some trouble come to you, I think, pretty soon, but the Lord will deliver you out of it." She said this with much earnestness and conviction, as if she had Divine light on the subject.

"My wife and I spoke of the matter as we walked back to the Mission. On the next day, or the next day but one, my wife became ill with pneumonia of an acute type, and came very near the gates of the grave, being very low for several weeks, but she recovered, just as had been said by this remarkable handmaiden of the Lord.

"I was never in my life so impressed with what seemed to be prophetic insight, as on this occasion."

SUNSET

In her early Christian life Ann had been taught to look upon death as the culminating point in Christian experience, ushering into all that was perfect. She had experienced the taking away of the sting of death, and one of her favourite utterances in her testimony was that "sudden death" to her would be "sudden glory." However, in her later life she had from the Scriptures had been taught to look for the personal return of the Lord Jesus, and it was to her a bright hope of the future. However, as the days and years flew by she sometimes became a little weary, and on several occasions again expressed her willingness and even desire, to depart and be with the Lord. The last few months of life, however, were full of great activity and constant witnessing. The Sunday before she passed away she was up as usual and present at the seven o'clock prayer meeting in the Berkeley Street Methodist Church. After her breakfast she went again to the class meeting and stayed for the preaching service. When the benediction was pronounced, she, with others, went up to say good-bye to the minister. Rev. Marmaduke Pearson, who was leaving for another charge. In her conversation with him she had not noticed that she had got up on the low platform, and gradually moving back, she stepped over the edge and fell with considerable force to the floor. However, she rose and did not seem to feel very much the worse for the little accident, and in the afternoon went out again to attend another meeting. Other than being somewhat wearied, there seemed to be no change when she retired to rest that evening, and she rose up as usual on Monday morning, took her customary bath, but just as she sat down to breakfast she was smitten with a stroke of paralysis.

She gradually sank into semiconsciousness. Mrs. Pedlow, the humble widow who had gladly shared her home with Ann during the last years of her life, was away at the time. She was immediately summoned home. During the intervening hours Ann lay with eyes wide open, but observing Mrs. Pedlow's arrival she seemed to be satisfied, and the weary eyelids closed.

For three days she lay perfectly still, and yet seemed to understand what was going on, for when asked to press the hand if she understood what was being said, or if she knew who was speaking, she would at once respond with gentle pressure. After lingering for a few days, she quietly slept away on Thursday, June 21st, 1906, at the age of 96. The sun was sinking in the west on the longest day of the year. Mrs. Pedlow and a few friends were watching by the couch. As the vital flame burned low, they sang softly:

"Abide with me, fast falls the eventide,
The darkness deepens: Lord with me abide;
When other helpers fail, and comforts flee,
Help of the helpless, O abide with me."

Just as the words, "Swift to its close ebbs out life's little day," broke the stillness of the room, the spirit quietly took its flight and the dear old saint was present with the Lord she loved. As soon as it was known, the home was thronged by hundreds anxious to get a last glimpse of the loved face, and on Saturday a fitting tribute was paid, when, in the Berkeley Street Methodist Church, the friends gathered to take part in the last services. The church was packed with friends, some of whom had come many miles to be present at that service. Ministers of six different denominations who had known her life paid fitting tribute in their testimony on this occasion to its influence and power in the lives of others. At the close of the service many followed to the cemetery at Mount Pleasant, where the body was interred. The earthly life has ended but its influence is still felt. Although her voice is no longer heard, this tribute to her memory is inscribed that the record of her words and deeds may continue to bring glory to the Father, with whom she lived in such intimate fellowship; to the Son, through the merit of whose blood alone she claimed redemption; to the Holy Spirit, by whose power she was quickened and kept; to the abounding grace of God, through which alone she was on earth what she now is in heaven,

"Holy Ann."

BILLY SPENCE
"A TROPHY OF GRACE"
BY JAMES GRUBB

❖

One of the songs Billy most loved to sing in the early days of his religious life was the song that began and ended with the words, "Glory to God, I've come home." And now that Billy has gone Home, how becomingly may we glorify God in him! For God's glory is God's grace, and the power of God's grace is the most impressive illustration of God's power we know. And never was the might of that power more impressively manifested than in seeking and finding and saving so notable and notorious a sinner as Billy Spence, who was born in Belfast and who died there on 21 January, 1924, aged 64 years.

HE WAS LOST

Of Billy it is only too true to say, "He was lost." He was lost to God. And as a consequence he was lost to everything and everybody else. A tragic and desperate condition to be in, as multitudes in every class of society well know. And that such a one as Billy should ever be found and saved, either by God or man, seemed at one time a thing incredible. For on the Shankill Road, Belfast, where he was born, he grew up to be a perfect terror to all who had to do with him.

Of course, that is to be explained in part by the fact that Billy grew up to be a confirmed and desperate drunkard. And drink it is that will transform even the best of men as into a very devil; and when Billy was in drink, and the drink was in Billy, he behaved like a fiend. The police were afraid of him. His encounters with them were terrific. Oftentimes it took three or four of them to get him to the police station. Down to his grave he bore in his body the marks of these frightful struggles. And when the time came, as come it did, when these same police touched their caps to him and said, "Good-day, Mr. Spence," his joy in his Lord was unbounded.

He had by nature, indeed, the instincts and capabilities of a pugilist. Fighting was an unholy joy to him. Years after his conversion, when a ministerial friend playfully put up his hands to Billy, in the attitude of a fighter, and Billy was about to respond, he suddenly dropped his hands, saying, "For God's sake don't do that to me again; you don't know what you do." Hence, in those wild and wicked years of his early manhood, Billy's degradation seemed complete. On one occasion, when home for a time from "the milishy", mad with drink, he jumped clean through the plate-glass window of a Shankill Road public house. And, of course, no methods were too low or too mean to adopt in order to obtain the money needed to secure the drink. For drink destroys all self-respect in men. Billy never spoke of these terrible years as if he gloried in his shame. On the contrary, the remembrance of them was a life-long sorrow to him, and though he often referred to them, he only referred to them that he might the more exultingly extol the wonder of Love that sought him and the grace that brought him home to God. So how often he would tell how he would hang about the precincts of the pawnbroker's shop until the pawnbroker had put up the shutters, and was putting out the lights. Then darting in with his bundle, as often as not one of his wife's garments, Billy would secure the price of a pint or two of porter, and hurry away before the pawnbroker could plainly see upon what a worthless pledge he had advanced his money.

O it is a pitiful state to be in, but Billy was in it! He was lost! Lost to purity, lost to sobriety, lost to society, lost to himself - lost to God! A drunken, fighting ruffian, he was a pest to society, a peril to the community, a problem to civilisation. As far removed, apparently, from godliness and usefulness as a man could well be, he seemed also, like many another, lost beyond the hope of recovery.

HE WAS FOUND

Nevertheless, Billy was found! He was gloriously and profoundly converted. He was re-born. It takes a God to do it, but blessed be His name, there is a God by whom it can be done! "His blood can make the foulest clean," and it cleansed Billy.

And how he loved to tell the story of it! And what countless thousands, at home and abroad, have heard him do so! And only the eternal years can disclose with what blessed results.

One fine spring Sunday afternoon, when he was now about 30 years of age, Billy was taking, as he used to say, "a careless dander" down by the Custom House steps. And in Belfast the Custom House steps has been for many years a great pulpit for the Gospel preacher. The preachers of the Belfast Central Mission, now established in the famous Grosvenor Hall, were holding their usual afternoon service there that Sunday, and Billy drew near in the throng to hear what the preacher had to say. Billy didn't know it was a religious service. He knew little or nothing about religion. The only religious service he ever attended was the service to which he was marched when up for training in "the milishy." He thought at first, he used to say, the young preacher was a doctor. But as the preacher reasoned that Sunday afternoon with this great congregation, and expostulated with them, on that occasion, on their habitual neglect on the Lord's Day of the Lord's House, Billy was rooted to the spot, and constrained to listen. And as he listened there came upon him as sense of awe and nameless fear. He became conscious of his sin and of the fear of God. God was speaking to him - even to him. And when at length, as he concluded his sermon, the preacher exclaimed, "O, men and brethren, would to God I could get you to give ten minutes to think about eternity!" Billy was overpowered. Eternity! Billy had never thought about anything except how to fight, and how to get drink. He began to think. He went home to think. Thinking, he passed a sleepless night. He sought guidance from his friends in vain, and for the two days and nights that followed he was a man in hell before the time.

Billy in those days was in charge of a "scow," a flat-bottomed barge that received the mud taken up and discharged upon it by the dredger to be taken out and re-discharged into the sea. And, unable any longer to bear up "under the tar'ble state" he was in, on the old mud scow, out in the Belfast Lough, all ignorant of what it was, exactly, he needed, Billy knelt down and began to pray. And he didn't pray long! If he didn't know what he needed, his Lord did. And He answered him. He came to him - came to Billy on that old mud barge, as alone, despairing, densely ignorant, without priest or preacher or prayer book, Billy called upon Him for relief and rest. There and then Jesus found Billy, and Billy found Jesus. And in finding the Lord Jesus Christ, Billy found freedom, and power and joy, joy that was as great as his distress had been great. His fears fled; his spirit was freed; and his whole being changed. He wept and sang aloud in strange, new joy, whilst, as he used to say, "the very 'say-gulls' flying over his head" seemed to be singing with him.

So Billy the lost became Billy the found. He was converted. There is no other word for it, and no other explanation of it. Of a very truth, he was re-born. What law, force, education, science, art, literature, cannot do for any man, though every man needs it done for him, God had done for Billy, as He will do it for each and for all. He had enlightened him, liberated him, forgiven his sin, and filled his heart with joy and peace.

Billy's manifestation of this change of character was wonderful. Love of drink and desire for fighting left him, and what is more, never returned. One day, not long after his conversion, he was going to Lisburn. As he sat in the corner of the railway carriage, almost unbearably happy, he began to sing softly, as to himself, what was for long his favourite chorus:-

"I'm on my journey up Zion's hill,
All the way long it is Jesus;
The way grows brighter and brighter still,
All the way long it is Jesus."

Whereupon a man half-drunk in the opposite corner of the carriage told him to "shut up" and upon Billy taking no notice of his command, crossed over and smote Billy a heavy backhanded blow upon the mouth. As Billy said to the writer, "It was a tar'ble moment." But a little while before Billy would have thrashed the wretched fellow helpless. As it was, he quietly wiped the blood from his lips - such power can God give unto man - and went on crooning his song:-

"Jesus! Jesus!
Why, all the way along it is Jesus!"

But if anyone ever did dispute the reality of his wonderful experience, there was one final argument Billy used to advance to confirm it, and that was - "If you don't believe me, ax Mary Ann." For "Mary Ann" was his wife! And that exhortation was for Billy then, as it always must be in this matter of the miracle of all miracles, the miracle of conversion, the end of all controversy. Moreover, himself lost and found, Billy had begun, as every converted man ought to begin to seek to find others.

HE FIRST FINDETH HIS OWN

And of course, "he first findeth his own." He became anxious for the conversion of is relatives, and especially for the conversion of Mary Ann.

Very touching, and always very tender was the way in which Billy used to speak of Mary Ann's worth, and her strange, strong devotion to him, even in his unregenerate days. There was a time when a relative of Mary Ann "wouldn't take him for an apronful of goold." But there came a day, said Billy many a time, when "Mary Ann wouldn't take an apronful of goold to get rid of him!" Such wonders love and grace can do! She marvelled greatly at the change that had come over her husband. She couldn't understand it. She only knew he was the same - yet not the same - man he had been. And so - no light task in a labourer's home, with little children to mind, she counted no labour too great to have the little kitchen ready for a Saturday night prayer meeting, and for yet another prayer meeting by eight o'clock on Sunday morning. Because Billy's home soon became a little Gospel hall, in which the songs and sounds of rejoicing were heard continually. So that little by little it dawned upon Mary Ann that, blameless as her own life appeared to be, she also needed this great salvation, and she also was "lost". For it is possible to be "lost" even though we appear to be, and, indeed may be, respectable and sober, and even churchgoing folk! And Billy became exceedingly concerned about the matter.

Mary Ann also became passed by the notion that perhaps God's messenger to her husband, and only he, could be God's messenger to her. So it came to pass, shortly after his conversion, Billy's leg was hurt, and one day after the writer had been with Billy in his own room, he returned to speak with "Mary Ann" downstairs, while Billy prayed upstairs. And it became a very easy and a very blessed task to tell Mary Ann, "the story simply as to a little child" - the old, old story of the wonderful redemption, God's remedy for sin. And she took it in; she received it simply and believed it firmly. And God found her, and made her quietly and deeply happy. She was never a boisterous believer, though always a true one. We are not all either born or re-born alike or in the same fashion. Enough that we know, and know that we know, as everyone may know, we are truly born of God, and have passed "out of death into life."

Mary Ann became a help-meet to Billy indeed! Gentle, refined, retiring, endowed with great common sense, as Billy struggled on and up she sustained and upheld him well. She wisely put no hindrance whatever in the way of his growing usefulness, though she greatly marvelled at it. She passed home to God in December 1913. And it was a wondrously blessed home-going. "I'm going, Billy, I'm going," was her frequent word. "Keep near to God, Billy, keep near to God." And when at length the time of her going was clearly just at hand, "I'm going to sing, Mary Ann," said Billy - for Billy had become quite a notable singer - "and if you know what I'm singing, raise your right 'hond'!" So Billy sang:-

"I'll love Thee in life, and I'll love Thee in death,
And praise Thee as long as Thou lendest me breath;
And say, when the death dew lies cold on my brow,
If ever I loved Thee, my Jesus, 'tis now."

And feebly, yet firmly, the right "hond" went up and Mary Ann went home.

Billy was by no means an attractive looking man the first time he attempted to tell in public his wonderful experience. He wore a huge muffler round his throat, had on a pair of white moleskin trousers, smelt most offensively of old "scow" mud, so that with his great spluttering, as he tried to speak, close proximity to him was not pleasant.

And when he was converted Billy could neither read nor write. Out of a big print New Testament Mary Ann "larned" him. And one Sunday afternoon at the Custom House steps, a spot very dear to Billy, a vast congregation stood spellbound as it watched him, like a little boy in an infant school, letter by letter, spell through St. John 1 and 12, and then shout aloud in praise to God, who had given the right "to such a mon as he" to become His child.

Hence, also, on the Shankill Road, and through all the city of Belfast and its neighbourhood, Billy became an extraordinary power for good. He was literally as a flame of fire wherever he went. The love of his Master constrained him, and the zeal of his Lord consumed him. He could not be silent on the great matter of his salvation. So that, after a few years, he was positively "thrust out" as an evangelist, and compelled to go anywhere and everywhere preaching the Gospel.

And nor tongue nor pen can tell with what wondrous results. For one thing, the converts of Billy's testimony are to be found in all grades of society, and were gathered in all grades of Churches. Elegant Churches and elegant people listened to him with respectful wonder and sympathetic appreciation. The common people - his own people - heard him gladly. Ministers of all denominations welcomed him as a companion and colleague. Calls for his words and work came to him from all parts of the kingdom. Twice he crossed the Atlantic and in the States and in Canada gathered many a sheaf into the garner of God. In the Cooke Presbyterian Church, Toronto, a work was done "unequalled since the days of Moody". For "oft when the word was on him to deliver" there was on Billy also, ignorant and unlettered man though he was, the great power of God. He had become a mighty man of prayer. He had direct and original dealings with his God. Walking through the fields near his home in Moira, a minister tells how he was arrested by the sound of a voice clearly uttering impassioned intercession. Looking over a hedge, he there saw Billy kneeling, his Bible open by his side, his hands clasped, and his eyes closed, pouring out his heart to God, far from the sight and sounds of men, seeking to be endued with "power from on high". So in his services, his truly eloquent and passionate witness to the grace and power of God was mighty indeed in its convicting and converting effects upon his hearers. He would speak of St. Paul, the conversion, as he would put it, of "the Devil's Postman," or like St. Paul before Agrippa, he would say, "I thank God I can speak for myself," and then invariably, at times in terms and tones of deep emotion, often humorously, with quaint shrewdness and piercing straightness, he would tell of the great day at the steps, and the great day on the "old scow," when to him also it was as if the heavens had been opened, and he, too, had see his Saviour and Lord, always clinching the whole matter with his oft-repeated, all-sufficient argument, "and if you don't believe me, ax Mary Ann."

Such incessant and strenuous labours, ranging over a period of nearly thirty years, in tent and hall, and at the corners of the streets, wore him out. His exhaustion sorely affected his throat and chest. So, murmuring, quietly as he had been wont to exclaim joyfully, "Praise the Lord," after a brief illness, at the beginning of 1924, he entered into rest.

Vast multitudes on his own singularly loved Shankill Road followed him to his burial in the Shankill Road Cemetery, sorrowing, even in their songs of rejoicing, that they should see his face no more.

"A brand plucked from the burning!" "A burning and a shining lamp for his Lord!" Unschooled and untaught as he was, he turned away to righteousness and shall shine as the stars for ever and ever.

Surely the Gospel of such grace and power as rescued Billy, and renewed Billy, and restored Billy to God and His Kingdom and His service, is the Gospel the world still needs, and we each require?

So:-

"Let me commend this Saviour to you,
The publican's Friend and Advocate too!
For you He is pleading His merits and death,
With God interceding for sinners beneath,
To save what was lost, from Heaven He came;
Come, sinners, and trust in Jesus' name;
He offers you pardon, He bids you be free -
If sin be your burden, O come unto me!"

And it shall come to pass that whosoever and wheresoever and howsoever any poor, lost, burdened soul shall call upon the name of the Lord, like as Billy called upon Him, on "the old mud scow" like Billy, he, too, shall be saved, and like him, go forth to save others.